Martin Nicholas Kunz . Patricia Massó

best designed

ecological hotels

avedition

Dolores

Les Cernieres

Lana, Meran

Lagarde

Mallorca

Dubai

Puerto Vallarta

Khao Yai

Yucatán

Riviera Maya

San Ignacio

Kichwa Tembo

Diani Beach

Mount Meru

Ngorongoro Crater

North Island

Etosha National Park

North Queensland

Yasawa

Tambopata

Damaraland

Wilson Island

Benguerra Island

Okavango Delta

Kruger National Park

Uluru

Plettenberg

Hermanus-Gansbaai

Wanaka

Torres del Paine, Puerto Natales

Here a chunky chair carved from a tree trunk. There a bed with a knobbly burlwood frame. Everywhere you look, roofs covered in reeds or palms. Where does the tent, the classic of close-to-nature travel, figure in this atmosphere of creativity? This book features tents of all shapes and sizes—a camp in the heart of the Australian bush, small, cozy "pods" in a snowy Alpine landscape and many other varieties. Welcome to the best designed ecological hotels. But let's just pause a moment to consider a legitimate flash of skepticism. Is it really possible to reconcile great

design and responsible tourism? And, if it is, is it really such a desirable combination? Or is this just a form of "muesli ecology" that denies our own aesthetic sense? Are we merely replacing one form of consumption with another...?
It is all the more important to deal with these concerns because they are well founded. As Albert Schweitzer, the "jungle doctor", once said, "We are life in the midst of life that wants to live". His statement—a simple, totally apt formulation of the ethical, harmonious relationship that can exist between human beings and nature—is an

excellent model for us today. Great sensitivity and care is required in our attitude to our environment, but we also have a duty to live the best life possible—precisely for the sake of the beautiful things in this world. This book presents a whole range of destinations that impressively combine two apparent contradictions—responsible ecotourism and luxury design. Some are in the Amazon rainforest, others in faraway parts of the South Pacific. There are those that feel like a back-to-nature expedition and others, closer to civilization, that demonstrate how in

03 04

tune with the environment modern luxury can be. Wood—one of the most primeval materials known to man—predominates, naturally. Contemporary, state-of-the-art technologies are also employed to protect the world's raw materials and vulnerable climate. But nobody should deny themselves the pleasures of fine cuisine and high-quality wellness treatments. Ecological considerations and world-class well-being are not necessarily mutually exclusive. Of course, if we choose to fly halfway around the globe to enjoy a holiday in harmony with nature,

questions will surely follow. But travel remains the best way of broadening the mind. It also shows that the responsible preservation of our natural environment is a necessity rather than a choice— for this, the world offers endless possibilities.

01 | Onguma Tented Camp

02 | Mowani Mountain Camp

03 | Kirimaya

04 | Jumeirah Bab Al Shams

Hier ein etwas wuchtiger Stuhl, der direkt aus einem Baumstamm herausgeschält wurde. Dort ein Bett, dessen Rahmen aus bizarr gewundenem Wurzelholz besteht. Und – hier wie dort – mit Reet oder Palmen bedeckte Dächer. Angesichts so viel purer Schöpferkraft darf der Klassiker unter den natürlichsten aller Reisen nicht fehlen: das Zelt. Auch davon mangelt es nicht an Beispielen in diesem Buch – sei es als Basislager mitten im Buschland von Down Under oder als kleiner, kuscheliger Kuppelbau auf den letzten Schneefeldern vor alpinen Gipfeln. Will sagen: Willkommen bei best designed ecolocigal hotels!

Allerdings stellt sich auch ein Zögern ein. So eine Art berechtigte Skepsis: Ja, geht das überhaupt zusammen? Hochwertiges Design auf der einen, verantwortungsbewusster Tourismus auf der anderen Seite? Und wenn: Ist das denn tatsächlich chic? Oder drängt sich hier unter dem Signum der Ökologie eine Müsli-Ästhetik auf, die auf jede Form von Annehmlichkeiten verzichtet? Drehen wir also den bösen Strom ab und greifen gleich zum Streichholz ...
Solche Bedenken liegen auf der Hand. Umso wichtiger erscheint es, sie aus dem Weg zu räumen. „Wir sind Leben inmitten von Leben, das

leben will", formulierte Albert Schweitzer einst so simpel wie präzise, um ethisch betrachtet Mensch und Natur miteinander in Einklang zu bringen. Das Statement des klugen Urwalddoktors taugt durchaus als Steilvorlage auch für die heutige Zeit: Denn bei allem notwendigen und sorgsamen Umgang mit der Umwelt gilt es, das eigene Leben ebenso gut zu gestalten – gerade auch um der schönen Dinge dieser Welt willen. So finden sich in diesem Buch eine ganze Reihe von Destinationen, die diese beiden Ansprüche – naturnahes, verantwortungsvolles Reisen sowie Design und Komfort der Extraklasse – auf beeindruckende

07 08

Weise verbinden. Sie führen in den Regenwald des Amazonas und in entlegene Winkel der Südsee. In ihrer Ursprünglichkeit lassen sie immer wieder das Gefühl einer Expeditionsreise aufsteigen. Oder sie zeigen, näher an der Zivilisation gelegen, wie umweltgerecht der Luxus der Moderne gelingen kann. Natürlich dominiert das Holz als einer der urtümlichsten Werkstoffe. Zugleich kommen neueste und modernste Techniken zum Einsatz, um die Rohstoffe und das bedrohte Klima dieser Welt zu schonen. Das bedeutet aber: auf die Freuden einer guten Küche und gepflegter Wellness muss niemand verzichten.

Ökologische Ansprüche und Wohlfühlen im Weltformat stellen so gesehen keinen Widerspruch dar. Klar, wer wegen eines naturgerechten Urlaubs um den halben Globus jettet, der wird sich Fragen gefallen lassen müssen. Doch andererseits bildet nichts mehr als Reisen. Umso schöner, wenn sie zur Einsicht führen, wie wichtig der verantwortliche Schutz unserer natürlichen Grundlagen ist. Denn dafür gibt es auf der ganzen Welt keine Grenzen.

dunton hot springs | dolores . colorado

DESIGN: George Greenbank, Katrin Henkel, Bernt Kuhlmann

Embark on a journey into the wilderness, back in time to the old Wild West—if you've found your way to Dunton Hot Springs you're either a nature lover or a soul in search of unbounded tranquility. Uninhabited for decades, this log cabin settlement was known as a ghost town until 1994. Situated at an altitude of 2,700 meters in the south-west of Colorado, it is surrounded by the endless wooded slopes of the Rocky Mountains, and boasts hot springs and a 10-meter high waterfall. Despite the occasional appearance by bears and moose, these log buildings are never short of bookings. Dunton Hot Springs' guests range from Hollywood VIPs to young couples on wedding packages. Can you imagine a more romantic way to start a life of wedded bliss? Cuddle by the fire, bathe in hot springs and enjoy exquisite gastronomic delights in the old saloon, which is now a restaurant and breakfast room. Real Wild West fans meanwhile, will prefer regional specialties such as elk meat, washed down with a hard drink at the bar. Dunton Hot Springs is a dream resort no matter what time of year. In winter guests can even go on snowshoeing or heli-skiing tours.

Eine Reise in die Wildnis, ein Trip in alte Wildwest-Zeiten – wer den Weg nach Dunton Hot Springs auf sich nimmt, ist entweder ein Naturliebhaber oder auf der Suche nach grenzenloser Einsamkeit. Als Geisterstadt machte die Blockhaus-Siedlung bis 1994 von sich reden. Denn jahrzehntelang hatte hier kein Mensch gewohnt – auf 2.700 Metern Höhe, im Südwesten des US-Bundesstaates Colorado. Ringsherum nur bewaldete Berghänge der Rocky Mountains, Quellen, ein zehn Meter hoher Wasserfall sowie Elche und Bären, die mal Guten Tag sagen. Dennoch: die Hütten, die heute als Gästezimmer dienen, sind gut ausgebucht. VIPs aus Hollywood kommen nach Dunton Hot Springs, aber auch junge Paare, die „Wedding Packages" buchen. Romantischer lässt sich kaum ein gemeinsamer Lebensweg beginnen. Kuscheln am Feuer, baden in heißen Quellen und edle Delikatessen im alten Saloon genießen, der jetzt als Restaurant und Frühstückssaal fungiert. Echte Wildwest-Fans bevorzugen natürlich regionale Gerichte wie etwa Elchfleisch und harte Drinks an der Bar. Dunton Hot Springs ist ein Traumresort und das ganzjährig. So bietet das Hotel im Winter seinen Gästen Touren mit Schneeschuhen oder Heli-Skiing an.

01 | Dunton Hot Springs guests stay in log cabins.
Holzblockhäuser bilden die Siedlung Dunton Hot Springs.

02   03

02 | Guests can even stay in tents.

Auch ein Zelt dient den Gästen als Quartier.

03 | Lounge and bedroom with open bathtub in the Wellhouse.

Wohn- und Schlafzimmer mit offenem Badezuber im Wellhouse.

04 | Expansive woodland surrounds the hotel complex.

Weitläufige Wälder umgeben die Hotelsiedlung.

05 | One of the rooms, complete with vintage wooden furniture and warm colors.

Ein Gästezimmer: warme Farben, altes Holzmobiliar.

04

05

verana | puerto vallarta . mexico

DESIGN: Heinz Legler, Veronique Lièvre

Ten years ago movie set designer Heinz Legler and decorator Veronique Lièvre began looking for somewhere to retire. At the end of their journey, they found the perfect spot, but instead of retiring, they designed and built Verana. The hotel is on Mexico's west coast overlooking the Pacific Ocean. Since November 2000 it has been welcoming visitors from all over the world who appreciate its seclusion and closeness to nature. There are eight detached bungalows, each individually designed and with its own name and theme. Some guests prefer accommodation with a strong, typically Mexican color scheme and the jungle outside the window; others favor a more restful interior decorated in the colors of the sea – white, turquoise and sea green. The hotel is perched on an exposed hillside and playfully incorporates the natural environment. There is, for example, a sparsely furnished, open-walled studio (palapa) offering panoramic views of the Pacific Ocean. The hotel's ecological philosophy is also reflected in the roof design, which uses jungle vegetation as covering. When something needs repairing, it is the local environment that provides the materials.

Der Filmausstatter Heinz Legler und die Dekorateurin Veronique Lièvre machten sich vor zehn Jahren auf die Suche nach ihrem persönlichen Ruhesitz. Am Ende ihrer Reise hatten sie den perfekten Ort gefunden, an dem sie sich aber nicht zur Ruhe setzten, sondern ihr eigenes Hotel planten und entwarfen. An Mexikos Westküste, direkt am Pazifischen Ozean, liegt das Gästehaus, das seit November 2000 Besucher aus aller Welt empfängt, die Abgeschiedenheit und Naturverbundenheit suchen. Acht eigenständige Bungalows können bewohnt werden, jeder ist individuell gestaltet, jeder trägt einen eigenen Namen und jeder ist mit einem eigenen Thema versehen. Mag der eine Gast einen Raum in landestypischen, kräftigen Farben und mit dem Dschungel vor dem Fenster, so schätzen Ruheliebende an einem anderen Haus das Interieur in den Farben des Meeres – von weiß über türkis bis meeresgrün. Das Besondere des Hotels ist, dass es die natürliche Umgebung spielerisch integriert und eine exponierte Lage am Hang hat. So gibt es ein karg möbliertes offenes Studio, auch Palapa genannt, das mit den weiten Fensterfronten einen herrlichen Blick auf den Pazifischen Ozean freigibt. Das ökologische Konzept der Herberge spiegelt sich auch am Bau der Dächer wider: Sie sind mit Dschungelpflanzen bedeckt. Wenn es irgendwo etwas auszubessern gibt, holt man das Ersatzmaterial einfach aus der Umgebung.

01 | The living space is open-plan, the roof covered with jungle plants.

Der Wohnraum kommt ohne Trennwände aus, das Dach wurde
mit Dschungelpflanzen bedeckt.

02 | Veranda rest area with a view of the Pacific Ocean.

Ruhezone auf einer Veranda, mit Blick auf den Pazifischen Ozean.

03 | One of the bungalow interiors—decorated in the colors of the sea.

Interieur in einem der Bungalows – gestaltet mit Farben des Meeres.

04 | Jungle plants and flowers surround the resort in Mexico.

Urwaldpflanzen und Blumen umgeben das Resort in Mexiko.

05 | Thanks to the mild climate, guests spend most of their time in the fresh air.

Dank milder Temperaturen verweilen die Gäste meist an der frischen Luft.

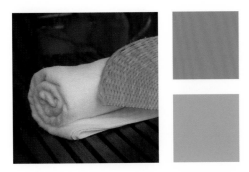

ikal del mar | riviera maya . mexico

DESIGN: Ramiro Alatorre

Despite the rapidly developing tourist centers, tranquil, luxurious holiday retreats can still be found on the Mexican Riviera between Cancún and Playa del Carmen. One coastal jewel not far from Playa del Carmen is the secluded Ikal del Mar hotel, whose name means "poetry of the sea". The open reception pavilion at the stylish private villa—with its hardwood floors, antique furniture and tastefully arranged plants—immediately reveals a fine attention to detail. There are twenty-nine spacious villas accessed by narrow paths that wind their way through ferns, banana plants, cacti and many other tropical trees and shrubs. The villas are a skillful blend of centuries-old Mayan traditions, modern luxury and contemporary technology. The focal point is the living and sleeping area with its dark, tropical wood floor, dining table, rattan couch and wicker chairs. The centerpiece is a large bed surrounded by a mosquito net. Large windows with slatted shutters for shade create the impression of bringing the natural surroundings into the room. Glazed doors or doors with fly screens provide seamless transitions between the indoor living area and the terrace with its sunken pool. Two circular buildings (separate for men and women) offer a sauna, a steamroom, a jacuzzi, massage facilities and a beauty salon.

Zwischen Cancún und Playa del Carmen an der mexikanischen Riviera gibt es trotz der sich dort rasch entwickelnden Touristenzentren noch genügend ruhige, versteckte Luxusparadiese. Nicht weit von Playa del Carmen entfernt liegt, ein abgeschiedenes Kleinod am Meer, das Hotel Ikal del Mar. Übersetzt bedeutet es „Gedicht des Meeres". Der offene Empfangspavillon der vornehmen Privatvilla – ausgestattet mit Edelholzböden, antiken Möbeln in archaischen Formen und fein arrangierten Pflanzen – verrät Sinn für geschmackvolle Details. Zwischen Farnen, Bananen, Kakteen, tropischen Bäumen und Büschen schlängeln sich schmale Pfade zu 29 geräumigen Bungalows. Sie sind eine geschickte Kombination aus jahrhundertealten Mayatraditionen und zeitgenössischem Komfort mit moderner Technik. In den Luxushütten dominiert der Wohn- und Schlafraum mit dunklen Tropenholzdielen, Esstisch, Rattancouch und Korbsesseln. Den Raummittelpunkt bildet ein großes Bett mit Moskitonetz. Großzügige Verglasungen mit schattenspendenden Lamellenläden schaffen unmittelbare Verbindung zur Natur. Die aus Glas oder mit Fliegengittern versehenen Türen verbinden den Wohnraum nahtlos mit der Terrasse und dem dort eingelassenen Pool. Zwei separate Rundgebäude für Männer und Frauen beherbergen Sauna, Dampfbad, Whirlpool, Massage und Kosmetik.

01 | The luxurious villas have dark tropical wood furnishings and
blend in perfectly with the natural surroundings.

Die edlen Hütten sind mit dunklem Tropenholz ausgelegt und
gehen nahezu vollständig in die Natur über.

03   04

02 | Each hotel villa has a private pool.

Zu jedem Bungalow des Hotels gehört ein eigener Pool.

03 | Large, comfortable beds are the focal point of the living and sleeping area.

Große bequeme Betten bilden den Mittelpunkt des Schlaf- und Wohnraumes.

04 | Wellness treatments are offered in two separate spa buildings.

Wellness-Behandlungen werden in zwei separaten Spa-Häusern durchgeführt.

azulik | riviera maya . mexico

DESIGN: Jorge Eduardo Neira & Holly Elizabeth Worton

As the moon is rising, you can either enjoy the bright moonlight or light candles. There is no electricity. On a clear night, the Milky Way seems close enough to touch. While taking an outdoor bath in the evening or in the morning, you have an endless view over the Caribbean. A wooden tub is built into the cliffs, the waves crashing against the rocks 15 feet below. If you know the white sandy beaches of the Riviera Mayas coastline, you know how unusual the topographical setting of the resort is. The outer reaches of the Sian Ka'an biosphere, protected by UNESCO, with its lush jungle vegetation meet the rare cliffs and white sandy bays and the off-shore coral reef, second only in size to the Great Barrier Reef in Australia. Only a few miles away, Mayan ruins proof that even this ancient civilization knew how special this place is. It is their only historical site with access to the ocean. Many visitors find it even more fascinating than the world famous Chichen Itza pyramids. Unlike typical Mayan stone structures, the buildings at Azulik are constructed out of locally grown logs that are woven together in an archaic style. Even the well-traveled visitor will be astonished to see this simple ancient architecture. While you are relaxing on a hammock under a mosquito net or on a wooden deck, you can easily forget about time and experience the true luxury of simplicity.

Wenn der Mond aufgeht, folgt man entweder seinem Schein oder zündet Kerzen an. Strom gibt es keinen. Dafür wirkt die Milchstraße bei wolkenlosem Himmel zum Greifen nahe und das abendliche oder früh morgendliche Bad im Freien bietet Endlosaussicht aufs Karibische Meer. Die Holzwanne ist in die Klippen montiert, Wellen klatschen rund fünf Meter tiefer auf Felsbrocken. Wer die meist flache Küste der Rivieria Maya mit seinen feinsandig weißen Stränden kennt, weiß wie exklusiv die topographische Lage dieses Resorts ist. Ausläufer der UNESCO geschützten Sian Ka'an Biosphäre mit ihrer Dschungel-Vegetation treffen auf hier eher seltene Felsenhügel, typisch weiße Sandbuchten und das vorgelagerte Korallenriff, das nach dem Great Barrier Reef das zweitgrößte der Welt ist. Nur wenige Kilometer entfernt zeugen auch die Ruinen der Maya von deren Wissen um gute Plätze. Es ist die einzige Stätte dieser Hochkultur, die sich am Meer befindet. Viele Besucher zieht das hier sogar noch stärker in ihren Bann als die bekanntere Pyramide von Chichen Itza. Im Unterschied zu den massiven Steinbauten der Maya haben die Konstrukteure des Azulik rohe Baumstämme der Region zu archaisch anmutenden Hütten zusammengeflochten; mit einem Ergebnis, das auch bei verwöhnteren Zeitgenossen Prickeln hervorrufen kann. Wer auf seiner Hängematte, dem Holzdeck oder im Bett unter dem Moskitonetz die Zeit vergißt, lernt den Luxus der Einfachheit zu genießen.

01 | Settled on a cliff between two beaches the 15 individual designed wooden-glass buildings offer both, stunning views and seclusion.

Einmalig exponiert ist die Lage. 15 individuelle Holz- und Glashäuser verteilen sich auf einem zum Meer mit Klippen abschließenden Hügel zwischen zwei Sandbuchten.

02 | 03 Highlight is the open-air tub in front of the wooden terrace, most of them are above the surge.

Ausgefallen sind die vor den Holzterrassen eingelassenen Freiluftwannen, die meisten „schweben" über der Brandung.

04

05

04 | Thatched roofs and wide open veranda doors provide air circulation, even if it's hot.

Spitz zulaufende Strohdächer und weit zu öffnende Türen sorgen auch bei Hitze für Luftzirkulation.

05 | Beside adobe walls the most is glass, covered with bamboo shutters.

Außer einigen Wandabschnitten aus Lehm ist der größte Teil des Gebäudes verglast, Schatten spenden Bambus-Rollos.

06 | Boardwalks between palm trees and rocks connect the villas, at night illuminated by candles.

Zwischen Palmen und Felsen winden sich die Holzstege, nachts sind sie mit Kerzen beleuchtet.

06

hacienda santa rosa | yucatán . mexico
DESIGN: team of architects

This 18th-century property is set in extensive grounds with lush trees. It combines genuine, old hacienda architecture with the luxury of a five-star hotel. The Spanish colonial influence is unmistakable. In the late 19th century this was a magnificent summer residence for a series of noble families and was also home to several hundred cattle, horses and mules. That colorful, eccentric culture has now been replaced by a total of eleven spacious rooms and suites. Rooms have a bedroom and a spacious bathroom. Some also have a terrace. Two of the junior suites share a section of the garden and a swimming pool with one of the especially generously proportioned deluxe suites. Another option is the Mayan Villa, which has a luxurious bedroom, a large terrace and other sumptuous features. Hacienda Santa Rosa has a restaurant, a bar, a massage room and a small library with books about Mayan culture and the flora and fauna of the Yucatán Peninsula. The surroundings offer some superb excursion destinations, such as the Ruins of Uxmal and a nature conservation area with a flamingo colony.

Eingebettet in ein großes, üppig bewaldetes Gebiet, vereint das bereits im 18. Jahrhundert erbaute Anwesen den Komfort eines Fünf-Sterne-Hotels mit der authentischen Architektur einer altehrwürdigen Hazienda. Die spanisch beeinflusste Kolonialarchitektur ist unverkennbar. Ende des 19. Jahrhunderts wurden hier noch mehrere hundert Kühe, Pferde und Maultiere gehalten. Das Anwesen diente damals als herrschaftlicher Sommersitz wechselnder adeliger Familien. Wo früher die bunte und oftmals exzentrische Gästeschar wohnte, sind heute die elf geräumigen Zimmer und Suiten untergebracht. Die Zimmer verfügen über einen Schlafraum, ein geräumiges Bad und zum Teil über eine Terrasse. Jeweils zwei Junior-Suiten teilen sich zusätzlich einen Teil des Gartens und einen Swimmingpool mit einer der Deluxe-Suiten, die besonders großzügig ausgelegt sind. Im Angebot steht zudem das Maya Landhaus, das unter anderem mit einem sehr geräumigen Schlafzimmer und einer weitläufigen Terrasse aufwartet. In die Hazienda integriert sind ein Restaurant, eine Bar, ein Massageraum und eine kleine Bücherei mit Literatur zur Mayakultur, Tieren und Pflanzen der Halbinsel Yucatán. Reizvolle Ziele laden zu Ausflügen in die Umgebung ein – etwa zu den Ruinen von Uxmal oder zu einem Naturschutzgebiet mit einer Flamingokolonie.

01 | Hacienda Santa Rosa combines modern luxury and historical charisma.

Die Hacienda Santa Rosa vereint historische Ausstrahlung mit modernem Komfort.

02 | A snooze in a hammock with views of the jungle-like surroundings.

Ein Nickerchen in der Hängematte mit Blick auf die dschungelähnliche Vegetation verwehrt hier niemand.

03 | The arcades, which are also an integral part of the pool, are architecturally stunning.

Architektonisch beeindruckend sind die Arkaden, die auch in den Pool integriert sind.

03

blancaneaux | san ignacio . belize

DESIGN: Manolo Mestre

Despite its proximity to Cuba, the small country of Belize is still relatively little-known. The fact that this Caribbean state barely registers in the consciousness of the world, makes the Blancaneaux resort seem all the more secluded. Situated amid the heights of the Maya mountains and surrounded by tropical forest, this natural paradise was discovered and created by none other than Hollywood director Francis Ford Coppola. Well-maintained roads take you past palm trees and tall forests to the „Refugium", which obtains up to 80 percent of its supplies from the resort's own gardens. This resort is framed by lush flora and fauna and also surrounded by 300 square kilometers of protected wilderness. Blancaneaux has seven different sizes of cabin, all built using natural construction methods. The tops of their bay-leaf-thatched roofs can be seen from far and wide. Fittings and furnishings in the villas and cabanas are comparable with Western standards, but the native-made handicrafts lend the houses a traditional charm. The hotel kitchen, meanwhile, serves classic Italian cuisine. A number of canoe and horse back riding tours are offered, each with their own individual appeal. Some even take you to remote caves, where the Maya once carried out their ritual ceremonies. Add the ethereal sounds emanating from the rain forest into the mix, and it's impossible not to feel just a little scared. After all, it's what Mr. Coppola would have wanted.

Belize ist ein kleines Land – im Grunde wenig bekannt, obwohl es Kuba unmittelbar gegenüber liegt. Und so verborgen wie dieser karibische Staat im Bewusstsein der Welt existiert, so fern ab erscheint auch das Resort Blancaneaux. Kein Geringerer als Hollywood-Regisseur Francis Ford Coppola entdeckte und erschuf das Naturparadies, das umsäumt vom Regenwald auf den Anhöhen der Maya Mountains thront. Gut ausgebaute Straßen führen entlang an Palmen und wuchtigen Bäumen hinauf zum Refugium, das sich zu 80 Prozent aus dem eigenen Garten versorgt. 300 Quadratkilometer geschützte Wildnis umgeben das, mit üppiger Fauna und Flora umrahmte Resort. Blancaneaux bietet Hütten in sieben verschiedenen Größen an, die allesamt in natürlicher Weise errichtet wurden. Sichtbares Zeichen: die Spitzen der Strohdächer. Die Ausstattung der Villen und Cabanas misst sich an westlichen Standards, die Küche kocht klassisch italienisch. Doch vor allem die indianischen Handarbeiten verleihen den Häusern einen ursprünglichen Charme. Einem eigenem Reiz haben auch die zahlreich angebotenen Touren mit Kanu oder zu Pferde. Teils führen sie zu entlegenen Höhlen, in denen die Mayas kultische Zeremonien abhielten. Wenn sich in diese Stimmung dann noch die unheimlichen Laute des Regenwaldes mischen, dann ist ein kurzes Schaudern nicht wirklich eine Schande. Coppola hat es so gewollt.

01 | The Francis Ford Coppola Villa in all its glory.
Ein Schmuckstück, die Francis Ford Coppola Villa.

02 | Indian handicrafts characterize the resort's cabins known as cabanas.

Indianische Handarbeiten bestimmen den Stil der Cabanas, den Hütten des Resorts.

03 | Some cabanas and villas have their own balcony.

Einige der Hütten und Villen warten mit einem eigenen Balkon auf die Gäste.

04 | Enjoy breathtaking views of the rugged highlands with their wild rivers.

Zweifellos traumhafte Ausblicke auf das zerklüftete Hochland mit seinen wilden Flüssen.

explora en patagonia | torres del paine . chile
DESIGN: Germán del Sol

Designed by the Chilean architect Germán del Sol, Explora en Patagonia lies in the Torres del Paine National Park, a UNESCO-listed biosphere reserve in Chilean Patagonia. It is ideally situated for extended trekking tours. Directly overlooking the shores of Lake Pehoé, this hotel is located at the foot of the 3,000-meter-high Paine Massif. With its functional exterior the building looks more like an alpine weather station than a luxury five-star hotel. Its strictly horizontal design, which serves as a counterpoint to the vertical slopes of the mountain, bears all the hallmarks of del Sol's work. These lines are also found in the façade's long, rectangular windows, which illuminate the hotel with narrow shafts of light. Inside, the motif is picked up again in the long foyer of what is known as the salon, and in the neighboring spa area. Almost all of the interior furnishings, including the wall decorations, carpets, fittings, furniture and lamps, are made from local cypress and lenga wood as well as slate and copper from local mines. With the tradition and precision you'd expect from hand-crafted goods, these superbly fashioned items are individually made for every one of the 50 rooms and suites.

Das vom chilenischen Architekten Germán del Sol entworfene Explora en Patagonia liegt im Nationalpark Torres del Paine, einem UNESCO-Biosphärenreservat im chilenischen Teil Patagoniens. Es ist Ausgangspunkt für ausgedehnte Trekking-Touren. Am Fuße von schroffen Dreitausendern des Paine Massivs und direkt über dem Ufer des Lago Pehoé gelegen, ähnelt das Gebäude mit seinem funktionalen Äußeren eher einer Wetter- oder Bergstation in den Alpen als einem komfortablen Fünf-Sterne-Hotel. Mit strengen horizontalen Gestaltungselementen als Kontrapunkt zu den Vertikalen des Gebirgsmassivs hat Architekt del Sol an dem Gebäude seine Handschrift hinterlassen. Diese Linien finden sich an der Fassade als Fenster in Form schmaler Lichtbänder und werden im Innenraum in der langen Flucht des so genannten Salons und im benachbarten Wellnessbereich wieder aufgenommen. Fast die gesamte Innenausstattung, wie Wandverkleidungen, Fußböden, Einbauelemente, Möbel und Lampen, besteht aus dem heimischen Holz von Zypresse und Südbuche (Lenga) sowie aus Schiefer und Kupfer regionaler Abbaugebiete. Alle Materialien wurden mit hohem gestalterischem Anspruch und in bester handwerklicher Tradition und Präzision verarbeitet und für die 50 Zimmer und Suiten individuell gefertigt.

02 | Interior furnishings made from cypress and lenga wood.

Für die Inneneinrichtung wurden Zypresse und Südbuche verarbeitet.

03 | Table lighting in the hotel dining room.

Tischbeleuchtung im Speiseraum des Hotels.

04 | Enjoy nature even when you're inside the hotel.

Die Natur findet sich auch im Hausinneren wieder.

05 | The architect del Sol arranged the windows to resemble bands of light.

Die Fenster hat Architekt del Sol wie Lichtbänder angeordnet.

remota | puerto natales . chile

DESIGN: Germán del Sol

Hotel Remota, which has only been open since 2005, occupies an exposed location by the ocean in the heart of the Seno de Ultima Esperanza province on the Chilean side of Patagonia. The architect Germán del Sol lets nature enjoy the limelight here—an abundance of glass surfaces and panoramic views provide it with the ideal stage. He found inspiration in the typical regional sheep stalls, where a lot of farming has to take place because of the harsh climate. In the spacious, centrally-located lobby that forms the heart of the hotel, guests are welcomed by warm, friendly yellows. Two side wings lead off from the main body of the hotel like outstretched arms. They house a total of 72 en suite rooms, all with telephones and individual safes. Each one has an unobstructed view of the surrounding scenery, which is stark and spectacular in equal measure. The landscape is dominated by the Balmaceda glacier, the Paine mountain range and the Ultima Esperanza bay. Your TV will not be missed. The sauna, indoor pool, restaurant and bar are perfect for recharging your batteries, and the hotel is an ideal base for excursions to southern Patagonia's largest city Punta Arenas, located directly opposite the Tierra del Fuego archipelago. It's also great for day trips and extended hikes in the nearby Torres del Paine National Park.

Auf der chilenischen Seite Patagoniens mitten in der Provinz Seno de Ultima Esperanza befindet sich in exponierter Lage, direkt am Ozean gelegen, das 2005 neu eröffnete Hotel Remota. Der Designer Germán del Sol hat der Natur den Vortritt gelassen und sie durch viele Glasflächen und Ausblicke in Szene gesetzt. Inspiration fand er bei den landestypischen Schafstallungen, in denen, bedingt durch das raue Klima, ein großer Teil des Farmlebens stattfindet. Warme, freundliche Gelbtöne empfangen den Gast in der zentralen, großzügig bemessenen Lobby, dem Herzstück des Hotels. Zwei Armen gleich führen die beiden Seitenflügel vom Hauptkörper des Gebäudes weg, in denen insgesamt 72 Gästezimmer mit privatem Bad, Telefon und eigenem Safe untergebracht sind. Jeder Gast kann von seinem Zimmer aus ungestört den Ausblick auf das umliegende Land, das karg und wunderschön zugleich ist, genießen. Der Balmaceda Gletscher, Paine Mountain Range Berge und die Ultima Esperanza Bay bestimmen das umliegende Landschaftsbild. Ein Fernseher wird hier nicht vermisst. Sauna, ein Indoor-Pool, Restaurant und Bar helfen zudem, sich an diesem Ort wohl zu fühlen. Sowohl kleine Reisen nach Punta Arenas – der größten Stadt im chilenischen Südpatagonien, welcher Feuerland direkt gegenüber liegt – als auch Tagesausflüge und längere Wanderungen in den nahen Nationalpark Torres del Paine bieten sich von hier aus an.

01 | Friendly colors and a welcoming atmosphere in the lobby.

Freundliche Farben und einladende Stimmung in der Lobby.

02 | 03 Remota Hotel is located on the shores of the ocean in Puerto Natales.

Das Remota Hotel liegt direkt am Ozean im Ort Puerto Natales..

03

04 | 05 Guests can enjoy so many stunning views across the
Ultima Esperanza Bay.

Überall eröffnen sich dem Gast herrliche Ausblicke auf die
Ultima Esperanza Bay.

reserva amazónica lodge | tambopata . peru

DESIGN: Denise Guislain

The Canopy Walkway—a series of swaying hanging bridges, towers and platforms woven through the green canopy of the rainforest—is an experience that no one ever forgets. Then there is the amazing wildlife that makes the Reserva Amazónica Lodge so unique. Tamarin monkeys, giant red squirrels, bright-colored toucans, screeching parrots, aras and so on—all clearly visible and rarely seen this close up in the wild. The Canopy Walkway at this private ecological reserve offers glimpses of the multicolored rainforest world that are normally the preserve of researchers. The lodge, which borders the Tambopata National Park in Peru, is also a research center. Life here is spartan—the cabanas (huts) have no electricity and the hot water comes from solar collectors. But the cabanas and other buildings are well equipped and their rustic, close-to-nature design is delightful. The amazingly wide river also adds to the idyllic picture. The most impressive aspect of the Reserva Amazónica Lodge are the opportunities (sometimes supported by researchers) to observe a variety of wildlife that is beyond the imagination.

Es ist schon ein bleibendes Erlebnis, wenn man über schwingende Hängebrücken, Türme und Stege durch das grüne Dach des Regenwaldes spaziert. So nah, so gut sichtbar, so unmittelbar in freier Wildbahn lassen sie sich selten beobachten, die schwarzen Äffchen mit ihren weißen Schnauzern, die übergroßen roten Eichhörnchen, die kreischend-bunten Tukane, Papageien, Aras und was es sonst noch so gibt. Das aber macht die Reserva Amazónica Lodge so einzigartig. Dieses private ökologische Reservat erlaubt mit seinem Canopy Walkway Einblicke in die sprichwörtlich bunte Welt des Regenwaldes, die sonst nur Forscher erhaschen. Denn die Lodge, die von der Lage her unmittelbar an den Tambopata Nationalpark in Peru angrenzt, besitzt eine eigene Forschungsstation. Und so herrscht hier durchaus ein spartanisches Leben. In den Cabanas, den zur Verfügung stehenden Hütten, wird auf Elektrizität verzichtet. Das fließend warme Wasser stammt von Sonnenkollektoren. Trotzdem sind die Hütten und Häuser großzügig aufgemacht. Sie verzücken durch ihren natürlichen Charme der rustikal-ursprünglichen Bauweise. Der unglaublich breite Fluss, der vorbei strömt, tut sein Übriges, um die Idylle komplett zu verklären. Doch am Ende beeindrucken vor allem die zahlreichen, teils von Forschern unterstützten Möglichkeiten, einer kaum bekannten Artenvielfalt auf die Spur zu kommen.

01 | There are three rows of detached huts.

Aufgereiht in drei Reihen steht jede
Gasthütte für sich.

01

02 03
04

02 | The life of a researcher—the mosquito net is a must, the hammock too.

Leben wie unter Forschern: Ein Netz gegen Moskitos ist obligatorisch, die Hängematte ebenso.

03 | Heavy furniture and tables made from huge rainforest trees.

Die wuchtigen Möbel und Tische entstammen den Baumriesen des Regenwaldes.

04 | The lodge restaurant serves tropical cuisine. The open roof creates a cathedral-like impression.

Das Restaurant der Lodge kocht tropisch. Das offene Dach wirkt wie eine Kathedrale.

05 | At night the paths around the camp are lit by candlelight and carbon lamps.

Nachts beleuchten Kerzenlichter und Karbonlampen die Wege des Camps.

castelnau des fieumarcon | lagarde . france

DESIGN: Frédéric Coustols

Lagarde lies on the edge of a mountain ridge in the Gascony region of France. Around 400 people lived here before the Second World War, but in 1975 was abandoned as the rural French flocked to the cities. These days the Gascony village of Lagarde is once again alive with the sound of people—Castelnau des Fieumarcon, its restored 13th century stronghold, is now a holiday village and venue for events and seminars. Lagarde is popular due to its rural charm, secluded location and mild climate, though it's almost worth coming just to see the striking simplicity of the architecture. The farmhouses and former stables, which now serve as accommodation and function rooms, look the same today as they did 80 years ago. Frédéric Coustols, owner of Lagarde and mastermind of the project, placed great value on maintaining the rural character of the village and its buildings. This means that the rooms, which currently number 27, feature stone floors, wide halls and old lattice windows as well as big farmers' beds and wooden tables. This country house style does away with the extraneous décor trappings usually found in hotels. Indeed, the lovingly fashioned bouquets of flowers—picked from the surrounded meadows and fields—are virtually the only bright colors in the houses. Visiting the many castles and palaces in the surrounding region is highly recommended.

Auf der Spitze eines Bergrückens der Gascogne liegt Lagarde. Vor dem Zweiten Weltkrieg lebten hier rund 400 Menschen. 1975 war der Ort verwaist – eine Folge der Landflucht in Frankreich. Heute kommen aber wieder Menschen nach Lagarde – als Hotelgäste, Seminarteilnehmer oder als Besucher von Veranstaltungen des Castelnau des Fieumarcon. Sie alle schätzen das milde Klima der Region sowie die Abgeschiedenheit und ländliche Idylle des Gascogne-Dorfes. Ein Grund hierher zu kommen, ist aber auch die Schlichtheit des Gebäude-Ensembles. Die Bauernhäuser und früheren Stallungen, die jetzt als Gäste- und Veranstaltungsräume genutzt werden, sehen noch so aus wie vor 80 Jahren. Der Eigentümer und Protegé des Projektes, Frédéric Coustols, hat Wert darauf gelegt, den ländlichen Charakter des Orts und der Gebäude zu erhalten. So finden sich in den derzeit 27 Gästezimmern überall Steinfußböden, breite Dielen und die alten Sprossenfenster genauso wie große Bauernbetten oder Holztische. Es ist ein Landhausstil ohne zusätzlichen Deko-Schnickschnack, der die Atmosphäre der Hotelanlage ausmacht. Die liebevoll dekorierten Blumensträuße – sie kommen aus Wiesen und Feldern der Umgebung – sind so ziemlich die einzigen Farbelemente in den Häusern. Als Tipp, in der Region gibt es viele Burgen und Schlösser zu bewundern.

01 | The traditional Gascony architecture of the houses has been preserved.

Die Häuser sind im Stil der Gascogne erhalten geblieben.

02

03

04

02 | Country house chic with wooden tables, upholstered furniture and bright and fresh flowers.

Landhausstil: Holztisch, helle Polstermöbel, frische Blumen.

03 | Doors and window shutters are completely preserved in their original form.

Türen und Schlagläden sind komplett erhalten geblieben.

04 | The rooms are furnished in an elegantly simple fashion.

Die Gästezimmer sind einfach ausgestattet.

whitepod | les cernieres . switzerland

DESIGN: Sofia de Meyer

Tents, great for getting close to nature. But let's be honest. Who really wants to schlep luggage and a tent nearly 3,000 meters up a mountain? There is an easier way. Camping up a snowy mountain just got a lot more fun—at Whitepod in the Valais, Switzerland. Whitepod has six igloo-shaped tents securely pitched on raised wooden platforms. The atmosphere inside is spartan yet cuddly—bedrooms equipped with petrol lamps, a woodstove and a bed. They serve merely as a place to sleep. The only luxury are huge windows that offer almost endless, panoramic views of majestic peaks and mountainsides piled high with snow. An old wooden Alpine chalet, often completely covered in snow, houses the bathrooms and a dining room serving regional dishes prepared using organic produce. If the design is rustic, the atmosphere is exceptionally cozy, especially the evenings in the lounge with its crackling log fire. During the day, winter sports are the attraction. Whitepod offers dog sled trips, snowshoeing and climbing tours through frozen landscapes. There is even a physiotherapist to massage away any stress. Et voilà! In 2005 Whitepod won an international award for innovation in responsible, sustainable tourism.

Nichts ist naturverbundener als Zelte. Nur ganz ehrlich: Wer möchte dafür schon Zelt und Gepäck fast 3000 Meter den Berg hoch wuchten? Das wäre dann wohl doch zuviel, oder? Das Whitepod im Schweizer Wallis ermöglicht nun dieses naturnahe Erlebnis. Auf Holzplateaus errichtete man sechs mit Streben geformte und gesicherte Kuppelzelte, in denen Holzofen, Schlummerbett und Petroleumlampen eine echt karg-kuschelige Atmosphäre verbreiten. Den Gästen dienen sie ausschließlich als Platz zum Schlafen. Luxuriös sind nur ihre großen Fensterluken, die den Blick fast endlos über tief verschneite Hänge und mächtig aufragende Gipfel schweifen lassen. Im Chalet, einem alten, oft völlig vom Schnee bedeckten Holzhüttchen, gibt es dazu die gemeinsam genutzten Baderäume und ein Gastraum, in dem ökologisch wie regional ausgerichtete Mahlzeiten serviert werden. Das Design ist rustikal, die Atmospähre urgemütlich. So wie die Lounge, in der bei knisterndem Holzfeuer der Abend ausklingt. Tagsüber locken in dieser hohen Region vor allem die Schneeaktivitäten. Das Haus bietet unter anderem: Hundeschlittenfahrten, Wanderungen mit Schneeschuhen und Klettertouren durch vereiste Landschaften. Auf Wunsch kümmert sich ein Physiotherapeut in einem Behandlungsraum um gestresste Körper oder Seelen. C'est tout! Den Machern von Whitepod trug es 2005 einen internationalen Award für Innovation im nachhaltigen und verantwortungsbewussten Tourismus ein.

01 | Covered in snow – Whitepod's domed
tents.

Tief verschneit: die Kuppelzelte von
Whitepod.

01

02 | Wooden platforms are a secure base for the tents, or pods.

Die Holzplateaus geben den Zelten, auch Pods genannt, einen sicheren Halt.

03 | A tent with an easy chair–the height of luxury! Perfect for admiring the view.

Ein Sessel im Zelt bedeutet schon Luxus. Der Blick hinaus ist dafür umso grandioser.

04 | Dreams are even sweeter in a high-altitude tent.

Über Wipfeln schläft es sich im Zelt noch verträumter.

vigilius mountain resort | lana . italy
DESIGN: Matteo Thun

Vigilius mountain resort is situated at an altitude of 1,500 meters amid the alpine splendor of the South Tyrol. This hotel, designed by the leading architect Matteo Thun, offers the very finest in nature and tranquility, and can only be reached by cable car. It is located on the mountain known as the Vigiljoch, where guests can enjoy awe-inspiring views of the Dolomites and the Adige Valley. Matteo Thun was inspired by the woodland, mountain lakes and rivers that surround the hotel. The interiors are made mainly from light-colored larch wood collected from nearby forests. It's also a key material in the exteriors, where the architect gives the art of wood-building a contemporary twist—for example by using wooden slats. There is a tangible closeness to nature throughout Vigilius mountain resort—guests can soak up the rays on the poolside sun terrace, or step out into the fresh air through the jacuzzi's sliding glass doors. Ecological aspects had a major role to play even in the design stage—the hotel is made mainly from glass and wood, which create optimum conditions for harnessing the sun's energy. The living area in all rooms and suites is seperated from the bathroom by a clay wall, which traps heat in the colder months and also helps regulate the atmosphere of the room. In 2005, the hotel was awarded a number of prestigious climate protection awards.

1500 Meter hoch, inmitten der Südtiroler Bergwelt, liegt das Vigilius Mountain Resort. Ruhe und Natur pur sind deshalb Markenzeichen des Hotels, das von Stararchitekt Matteo Thun geplant wurde und nur mit einer Seilbahn zu erreichen ist. Wer hier oben – auf dem sogenannten Vigiljoch – verweilt, genießt eine beeindruckende Aussicht auf die Dolomiten und das Etschtal. Rund um das Hotel befinden sich Wälder sowie Bergseen und Bäche. Matteo Thun hat sich davon inspirieren lassen. Vor allem helles Lärchenholz aus der Umgebung findet sich im Interieur wieder, aber auch als Material für die Außenfassade. Dort hat der Architekt die Kunst des Holzbaus zeitgemäß umgesetzt – etwa in Form von Holzlamellen. Die Einbindung der Natur zieht sich durch das ganze Vigilius Mountain Resort: So schließt sich dem Hotelpool eine Sonnenterrasse an, und vom Whirlpool aus gelangen Badegäste durch eine gläserne Schiebetüre ins Freie. Bereits in der Konzeptionsphase des Berghotels spielten ökologische Aspekte eine große Rolle: Glas und Holz als dominierende Baustoffe garantieren eine optimale Nutzung des Sonnenlichts zur Energiegewinnung. In den Zimmern und Suiten trennt eine Wand aus Lehm den Wohnbereich vom Bad. Sie schafft in der kalten Jahreszeit Wärme und reguliert zudem das Raumklima. Im Jahr 2005 wurde das Hotel deshalb mit bedeutenden Klimaschutz-Preisen ausgezeichnet.

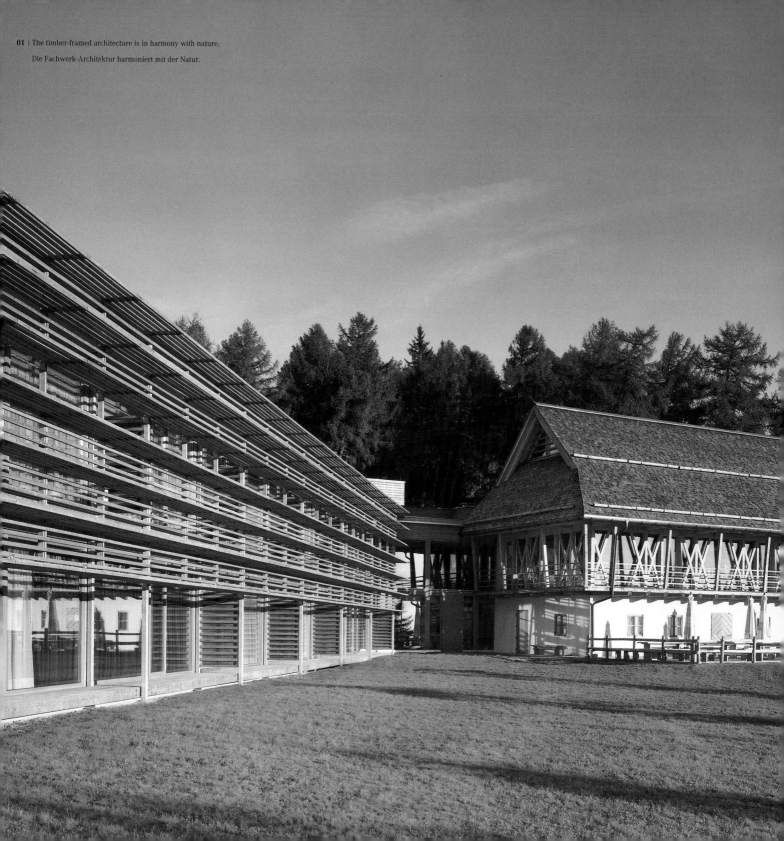

01 | The timber-framed architecture is in harmony with nature.

Die Fachwerk-Architektur harmoniert mit der Natur.

02 | Larch wood gives the dining room a light, airy appearance.

Lärchenholzgebälk im Speisesaal schafft Helligkeit.

03 | The floor of the swimming pool is inlaid with smoky quartz from Vipiteno.

Der Pool-Boden ist mit Silberquarz aus Sterzing ausgelegt.

01 | The natural stone ascent to the Pergola Residence.

Der Aufgang zur Pergola Residence aus Naturstein.

pergola residence | meran . italy

DESIGN: Matteo Thun

The Pergola Residence is an architectural jewel in the heart of the South Tyrol. Designed by the architect Matteo Thun, it blends in perfectly with its natural surroundings. Every apartment has generously sized rooms that enjoy plenty of natural light, as well as a spacious 40 square meters terrace that offers stunning panoramic views of the scenery. Let your gaze wander for too long and you'll feel as if you're floating on the mountain air. There is also a roomy living area, and each apartment has a bath, a separate WC, a kitchen and its own entrance. Dividing walls between the terraces are made exclusively from natural materials such as wood, wicker, glass and natural stone. The Pergola Residence is a shining example of Matteo Thun's unashamed pursuit of his "ecotecture" philosophy, where he reduces architecture to the simplest terms possible. Elegant structures without the usual flourishes and unnecessary pomp draw the eye with their clear, defined shapes. This extraordinary complex also has a pool and sauna, and there's lots to see and do in the surrounding region. It is also an ideal place for work and for drawing inspiration from the beautiful scenery. All the necessary technical facilities are available, and the relaxing, tranquil atmosphere provides the perfect conditions for creative thinking. The complex blends perfectly with its natural surroundings.

Mitten in Südtirol hat der Architekt Matteo Thun mit der Pergola Residence ein Kleinod der Architektur geschaffen. Eingebettet in die Natur verschmilzt die Anlage mit ihrer Umgebung. Unbezahlbar ist wohl der freie Blick von der 40 Quadratmeter großen Terrasse, den natürlich jede Wohnung besitzt. Licht durchflutet die großzügig geschnittenen Räume. Den Blick schweifen lassend hat man das Gefühl völlig frei zu atmen. Neben Bad, abgetrenntem WC, Küche und einem eigenen Eingang, gewinnt der große Wohnbereich das Herz des Gastes. Der Architekt nutzt ausschließlich natürliche Materialien, wie Naturstein, Holz, Weidengeflechte und Glas für die Abtrennungen der Terrassenflächen. Die Reduktion auf das Wesentliche, die Natur, ist das offensichtliche Credo des Architekten, das er hier auch konsequent umsetzt. Elegante Formen ohne Schnörkel und überflüssigen Prunk bieten dem Auge klare, übersichtliche Strukturen. Den Gästen dieser außergewöhnlichen Anlage stehen Sauna, Pool und die Freizeitangebote der näheren Umgebung zur Verfügung. Dieser Ort ist auch ideal, um zu arbeiten und sich von seiner Umgebung inspirieren zu lassen. Die notwendige technische Ausstattung ist selbstverständlich vorhanden; sowie die entspannte, ruhige Atmosphäre, die eine perfekte Grundlage für neue kreative Einfälle schafft. Die Einbettung in die Natur ist perfekt gelungen.

02 | Hidden away, yet exposed—Pergola Residence's location offers panoramic views of the Adige Valley and the Alps.

Die versteckte und doch exponierte Lage der Residence gibt den Blick ins Etschtal und in die Alpen frei.

03 | 04 | 05 | 06 Apartments are furnished to the highest standards with all creature comforts.

Die Wohnungen sind mit allen Annehmlichkeiten auf qualitativ höchstem Niveau ausgestattet.

03

04

05 06

01 | Guests are greeted by the interplay of light and shade. The hotel is reminiscent of an old Mallorcan manor house.

Ein Zusammenspiel von Licht und Schatten empfängt den Besucher. Die Gebäude erinnern an ein altes Hofgut auf Mallorca.

son bernadinet | mallorca . spain

DESIGN: Antonio Esteva

A small sign "Agritourismo Son Bernadinet" on the road between the Mallorcan villages of Porreres and Campos points the way to this historical, Mallorcan property, from whose 200-year-old undressed stone walls local architect Antonio Esteva has lovingly created a hotel in the style of a country house. Stepping through the steel columns at the main entrance is like walking into a friend's elegant home. The hotel is especially beautiful at dusk, when bright light streams through the windows and doors. The clarity of form continues in the interior, right down to the last detail, with white, brown and beige the predominant shades. How many rooms? The main building has four spacious bedrooms grouped as a unit and there are a further seven bedrooms. For families with children, this Mallorcan country hotel offers well-appointed accommodation and plenty of space. Proprietor Francisca Bonet and daughter Alicia Fernández introduce guests to the local cuisine and the history of Mallorca. True to the hotel's ecological credentials, guests gather beneath the age-old olive trees in front of the house to savor a cabernet sauvignon from Jaume Mesquida's vineyard at Porreres.

Zwischen den beiden Orten Porreres und Campos auf Mallorca, direkt an der Verbindungsstraße, weist ein kleines Schild „Agritourismo Son Bernadinet" den Weg zu dem historischen, mallorquinischen Gemäuer. Aus dem 200 Jahre alten Bruchstein gestaltete der ortsansässige Architekt Antonio Esteva behutsam ein Hotel im Landhausstil. Wer durch die stählernen Pfeiler des Hauptportals schreitet, fühlt sich, als besuche er das Gutshaus eines Freundes. Besonders in der Dämmerung ist es schön, weil helles Licht durch Fenster und Türen nach draußen strahlt. Die klare Formensprache setzt sich im Innern des Hotels fort – bis ins kleinste Detail. Weiß, Braun und Beige sind die dominierenden Farben. Wie viele Zimmer können bewohnt werden? Im Haupthaus liegen vier große Schlafzimmer, die eine Einheit bilden. Außerdem gibt es sieben weitere Gästezimmer. Das Landhotel auf Mallorca bietet viel Raum für Familien mit Kindern, die Behaglichkeit auf großzügiger Fläche wünschen. Die Gastgeber Francisca Bonet und Tochter Alicia Fernández vermitteln den Gästen die einheimische Küche und die Geschichte Mallorcas. Zum ökologischen Konzept gehört auch, dass sich die Gäste unter steinalten Olivenbäumen vor dem Haus treffen und einen Cabernet Sauvignon aus der Weinkellerei von Jaume Mesquida in Porreres genießen.

02 | One of the eleven bedrooms with white fabrics and a ceiling of light wood.

Eines von elf Schlafzimmern mit weißen Stoffen und einer hellen Holzdecke.

03 | An open staircase leads to the guestrooms.

Eine offene Treppe führt nach oben zu den Gästezimmern.

04 | Simple decor, plenty of light and a comfortable sofa—rooms designed for relaxation.

Wenig Interieur, viel Licht und ein bequemes Sofa - die Zimmer laden zum Verweilen ein.

04

kirimaya | khao yai . thailand
DESIGN: ISM & Februar Image

Kirimaya is a Siamese word that means "the illusion of mountains". The name refers both to the philosophy behind this luxury golf resort, and to its location amid the towering peaks of Thailand's oldest nature park, a scenic idyll of evergreen grasslands and hills. Kirimaya was built on the fringes of this natural paradise in 2004. It isn't just a retreat for well-heeled businessmen from Bangkok though; its contemporary design and golf course designed by Jack Nicklaus, attract visitors from all over the world. Alongside the 52 rooms and four suites, there are four tented villas, which offer every comfort imaginable, including a private spa pool. Designed in the style of a traditional rice barn, the pavilion that houses the resort's "Acala" restaurant appears as if it is floating on the lake. There are so many ways for nature lovers to explore Kirimaya's surroundings, including trekking tours through the unspoilt wilderness and tours of the nearby vineyards. Those in search of relaxation can take advantage of a number of oriental therapies, perfect for restoring balance to mind and body. Meanwhile, the Kirimaya Sutra lifestyle experiences have a whole host of surprises in store for guests...

Kirimaya ist siamesisch und bedeutet „Die Erscheinung der Berge". Namen sind zwar Schall und Rauch. Doch in diesem Falle steht er sowohl für die Lage des Luxus Golf Resorts wie für die Philosophie des Hauses. Was heißen soll: In Thailands erstem und einzigem Naturpark erheben sich stolze Gipfel. Der Park selbst ist ein landschaftliches Idyll aus immergrünem Grasland und Hügeln. Am Rande dieser Oase wurde 2004 Kirimaya errichtet – ein Ort zum Rückzug nicht nur für betuchte Geschäftsleute aus Bangkok. Zeitgemäßes Design und ein Golfplatz, der von Mastersieger Jack Nicklaus gestaltet wurde, locken auch internationale Liebhaber eines natürlichen „Hideaways" an. Dafür stehen 56 Räume zur Verfügung, zudem vier Suiten und als luxuriöse Highlights 180 Quadratmeter große Villen, die wie Zelte erscheinen. Sie bieten neben allem Komfort einen eigenen Spa-Pool. Der Pavillon, der das Restaurant Acala des Resorts beherbergt, scheint derweil wie über Wasser zu schweben und ist einer traditionellen Reisscheune nachempfunden. Naturfreunde finden in Kirimaya viele Möglichleiten die Umgebung zu erkunden: Trekking-Touren durch die unberührte Wildnis und Führungen durch nahe Weinberge. Wer die Entspannung sucht, dem sind die zahlreichen asiatischen Therapien zu empfehlen, die Körper und Geist wieder in Einklang bringen. Man frage nur nach den Angeboten des Kirimaya Sutra...

02 | Bamboo beds and rattan weaving add a natural touch to the contemporary design.

Bambusbetten und Rattangeflechte sprechen eine natürliche Sprache im zeitgemäßen Design.

03 | Kirimaya at night—a two-story jewel surrounded by water and rich natural scenery.

Kirimaya bei Nacht – ein zweistöckiges Kleinod inmitten von Wasser und satter Natur.

04 | Restaurant Acala combines modern and traditional styles, and serves exquisite Thai cuisine.

Das Restaurant Acala: traditionell und modern zugleich gestaltet. Serviert wird feine thailändische Küche.

05 | All four suites have spacious terraces. This romantic idyll is the place where to write your postcards.

Alle vier Suiten bieten geräumige Terrassen. Ein romantisches Idyll: Der Platz für die Reisepost.

voyages coconut beach rainforest lodge | north queensland . australia
DESIGN: Watermark

Daintree Forest Nature Reserve in Australia's Northern Queensland region is a UNESCO World Natural Heritage Site. It's not difficult to see why either – indeed it can boast 85 species of plants that are recognized as being among the rarest in the world. Tucked away in the foothills of this nature reserve is Coconut Beach Rainforest Lodge, a tropical-style ensemble with all the comfort you would expect from a four-star establishment. Its private beach is on the fringes of the Great Barrier Reef, and also marks the beginnings of a UNESCO-protected biosphere reserve. With lots to see and do in the water and on land, the location is perfect for adventurous outdoor types. Crocodiles come just shy of snapping-distance on boat trips through the meandering waterways of the mangrove forests, while canoes or sailing boats can take you to fascinating diving spots in a matter of minutes. Night-time walks, meanwhile, offer a whole new way of experiencing the dense forests. You can even roll your sleeves up and help the rangers with their conservation work. Coconut Beach Rainforest Lodge has two different types of accommodation—the Daintree Retreats are the epitome of elegant simplicity, while the aptly named Rainforest Retreats boast cozy surroundings made from natural materials. The secluded location of these retreats makes them an ideal listening post for the serene sounds that precipitate from the rainforest.

Das Naturreservat Daintree Forest im nördlichen Queensland von Australien gehört zum Weltnaturerbe der UNESCO. Der Grund dafür liegt auf der Hand: Der Park beheimatet allein 85 Pflanzenarten, die zu den seltensten der Welt zählen. In die Ausläufer dieses Naturreservats eingebettet liegt die Voyages Coconut Beach Rainforest Lodge – ein tropisch anmutendes Ensemble mit eigenem Strand und vier Sterne Komfort. Vom Strand des Hauses aus beginnen die ersten Korallenriffe des Great Barrier Reefs – ebenso Teil der von der UNESCO geschützten Biosphären. So scheint der Ort wie geschaffen für erkundungsfreudige Naturreisende, sei es nun zu Wasser oder zu Lande. Bei Schiffstouren durch die verschlungenen Kanäle der Mangrovenwälder kommen Krokodile zum Greifen nahe. Per Kanu oder Segelboot sind in wenigen Minuten faszinierende Unterwasserwelten zu erreichen. Wanderungen in der Nacht lassen das Erwachen des Urwaldes erleben. Oder man fügt sich nützlich ein und hilft den Naturschützern beim Erhalt des Parks. Als Herberge bietet die Lodge zwei unterschiedliche Unterkünfte: Im Daintree-Retreat herrscht nüchterner Purismus vor, die Rainforest Retreats stehen für sich und spielen romantisch anheimelnd mit naturnahen Materialien. Dank der vereinzelten Lage wirken sie wie wohnliche Ohrmuscheln, ausgefüllt von der reichen Geräuschkulisse des Regenwaldes – und somit garantiert lauschig.

02 | The simple yet extremely comfortable furnishings of the Daintree Retreats.

Die Ausstattung der Daintree Retreats ist bemerkenswert nüchtern, bietet aber dennoch viel Komfort.

03 | Get close to nature in the Rainforest Retreats with their panoramic views over the lush scenery.

Eine naturnah gestaltete Oase mit freiem Blick auf die üppige Fauna: die Rainforest Retreats.

daintree eco lodge & spa | north queensland . australia
DESIGN: Cathy and Terry Maloney

Daintree Eco Lodge & Spa is tucked away in an area of rainforest that is over 100 million years old. Situated in Daintree National Park on the east coast of Australia, this small hotel retreat is within easy reach of the Great Barrier Reef, just one of the many natural wonders this region has to offer. Accommodation is provided by 15 basic tree houses, so don't expect a conventional luxury resort. The people behind the retreat wanted to make as little impact as possible on this unspoilt natural scenery, ensuring the rainforest's flora and fauna could develop as nature intended. The houses stand on stilts, and are connected to each other and to the restaurant by a system of raised walkways. Reminiscent of safari lodges, the interiors can only be described as simple and functional, with wooden furniture, subdued natural tones, and light, airy materials. Everything about the resort has been designed to provide guests with an intense, "close-to-nature" experience. This includes the food (made with locally sourced nuts, roots, fish and exotic fruits), the wellness area with its own body-care products, and the excursions in the surrounding countryside and to the Great Barrier Reef. It represents the realization of a broad ecological concept that has two key aims—to provide intensive experiences of the almost totally unspoilt nature, and to give in-depth insights into authentic Aboriginal culture.

An der Ostküste Australiens, im Daintree Nationalpark, liegt in einem über 100 Millionen Jahre alten Stück Regenwald eine kleine Hotelanlage – die Daintree Eco Lodge & Spa. Der Wald grenzt direkt an das Great Barrier Reef, ein weiteres Naturwunder dieses Landstrichs. Das Hotel mit 15 einfachen Holzhütten ist mit einem exklusiven Resort nicht zu vergleichen. Den Betreibern ist wichtig, den Eingriff in die ursprüngliche Natur möglichst gering zu halten – dadurch kann sich Flora und Fauna des Regenwaldes ungehindert entfalten. Die Hütten stehen auf Stelzen und sind sowohl untereinander als auch mit dem Restaurant über Stege verbunden. Wie ist die Inneneinrichtung gestaltet? Schlicht und zweckmäßig, sie erinnert an den Safaristil: Holzmöbel, gedeckte Naturtöne, leichte und luftige Stoffe. Das gesamte Angebot des Hotels ist darauf ausgerichtet, den Gästen ein intensives Naturerlebnis zu ermöglichen. Dazu gehört das Essen (exotische Früchte, Nüsse, Wurzeln und Fische der Region), ein Wellness-Zentrum mit eigenen Bodycare-Produkten sowie Ausflüge in die nähere Umgebung oder zum Great Barrier Reef. Das Resort realisiert ein ganzheitliches, ökologisches Konzept mit zwei Hauptkomponenten: intensives Erleben einer nahezu unberührten Natur und das unmittelbare Kennenlernen der authentischen Kultur der Aborigines.

01

01 | The Daintree Eco Lodge hotel resort is located in the heart of the rainforest.

Mitten im Regenwald liegt die Hotelanlage Daintree Eco Lodge & Spa.

02 | The covered spring-water pool with its summer terrace.

Der überdachte Pool mit Quellwasser und die angrenzende
Sommerterrasse.

03 | A tree house blends in perfectly with its surrounding ecosystem.

Eine Pfahlhütte, umgeben von einem intakten Ökosystem.

voyages wilson island | wilson island . australia

DESIGN: Pike Withers

Azure blue waters lap around this island, which is part of the Great Barrier Reef, a world heritage site. In the twilight, turtles crawl up onto the shore and, when confident they are not being watched, bury their gleaming white eggs in the sand. They also care for their brood once they have hatched. Wilson Island is a natural paradise and one of few islands to restrict the length of guest stays—the conservation of its natural beauty is the absolute priority. Visits are limited to three days and are combined with a stay at the nearby Heron Island Resort. The accommodation on Wilson Island consists of just six permanent tents with thatched roofs. Their open, modern design is stunning, but guests expecting electricity are in for a disappointment. In the evenings light is provided by battery. Shower water is heated by solar power. Wilson Island offers a rare luxury—freedom from technology—and is not a place for cellphones. Instead there are opportunities to explore—with care and sensitivity—a fascinating underwater world and discover the island's turtles and birds. Guests can also enjoy the healthy food provided at the resort, happy in the knowledge that nature is sometimes simplicity itself.

Azurblaues Wasser umspült die Insel, die zum Weltnaturerbe des Great Barrier Reef gehört. Schildkröten robben hier zuhauf an Land. In der Dämmerung, wenn sie sich unbeobachtet fühlen, verbuddeln sie im glitzernd weißen Sand ihre Eier. Um die Brut kümmern sie sich, sobald sie geschlüpft ist. Wilson Island ist ein Naturparadies. Als eine der wenigen Inseln erlaubt sie den Aufenthalt nur für eine begrenzte Zeit, denn der Schutz dieses natürlichen Kleinods besitzt uneingeschränkten Vorrang. Daran müssen sich die Drei-Tages-Besucher strikt halten. Vom benachbarten Heron Island Resort aus besteht für sie die Möglichkeit, sich in eine der nur sechs vorhandenen Hütten einzumieten. Die mit Reet gedeckten und offen gestalteten Behausungen erstaunen zwar durch ihr modernes Design, doch wer deshalb Stromversorgung erwartet, wird enttäuscht. Batterien sorgen für abendliches Licht, dank Solartechnik fließt aus den Duschen warmes Wasser. Wilson Island bietet den seltenen Luxus, sich mal von allen technischen Errungenschaften zu befreien. Selbst Handys wirken da störend. Dafür gibt es Gelegenheit, in eine faszinierende Unterwasserwelt abzutauchen oder mit aller Vorsicht den Schildkröten und Vögeln der Insel nachzustellen. Oder man erfreut sich schlicht an der gesunden Versorgung des Resorts. Die simple Erkenntnis davon könnte sein, dass es die Natur manchmal ganz einfach mit einem meint.

01 | Wilson Island is an uninhabited natural paradise.

Wilson Island ist ein unbewohntes Naturparadies.

02 | The tents are stylish. There is running water but no electricity.

Die Einrichtung der Hütten beweist Chic. Es fließt nur Wasser, dafür kein Strom.

03 | Natural materials predominate.

Natürliche Materialien dominieren das Mobiliar.

voyages longitude 131° | uluru . australia
DESIGN: Philip Cox

Vovages Longitude 131° is situated in the heart of the expansive, seemingly never-ending wilderness of the Australian outback, which is shrouded in the myths of its aboriginal inhabitants. You'll know you've reached this haven when you spy Ayers Rock, or Uluru as the Aborigines call their sacred monolith. Longitude 131° is situated directly facing this world-famous red colossus. The resort can only be described as a campsite that has been transported onto a vast sand dune—its 15 luxury tents are lined up next to each other like a marching army. The resort captures the spirit of the pioneers and has no need for any concrete constructions. It makes an excellent base camp for tours of discovery through the arid bushland of Kata Tjuta National Park. The caves and cascades of Ayers Rock are just a quick march away, not to mention the cultural monuments of the Anangu, the indigenous aboriginal people. These canopied villas offer ample protection from the cold outback nights, and they're astoundingly luxurious—a mix of colonial British stylings and traditional art and handicrafts. The resort's bar and restaurant are great places to meet other explorers and swap stories, and walkers can refuel with French-Australian dishes, which can also be served in the middle of the outback under the star-speckled southern night sky.

Schon der Name spricht Bände: Wie eine lose Positionsbestimmung gibt er den Ort an im schier endlosen Outback von Australien, jener grenzenlos weiten Wüste mit ihren von Mythen umrankten Ureinwohnern. Ja, wäre da nicht Ayers Rock – oder Uluru, wie die Aborigines ihren heiligen Monolithen nennen – der gleichermaßen als Markierungspunkt dient. Diesem weltberühmten roten Koloss direkt gegenüber liegt Longitude 131°: Ein Resort wie ein Zeltlager, das auf einer großen Sanddüne platziert wurde und das mit seinen 15 Villenzelten aufgereiht erscheint wie an einer Schnur gezogen. Das Resort spielt bewusst auf den Pioniergeist an und verzichtet gezielt auf Bauten aus Beton. Wie ein Basislager dient es für Erkundungstouren durch das dürre Buschland des Nationalparks Kata Tjuta. Nur einen Fußmarsch entfernt warten die Höhlen und Kaskaden von Ayers Rock, ganz zu schweigen von den Kultstätten der Anangus, dem heimischen Stamm der Region. Schutz für die immer wieder auch kalten Nächte bieten die villenartigen Zelte. Sie sind erstaunlich luxuriös ausgestattet – ein Mix aus Kolonialstil, sehr britisch anmutend, und althergebrachter Kunst und Handarbeiten. Restaurant und Bar des Resorts dienen nicht nur als Treffpunkt zum Austausch unter Naturtrekkern. Die Küche stärkt die Wanderer mit französisch-australischen Gerichten und serviert auf Wunsch mitten im Outback unter den Sternen des Südens.

ROYAL FLYING DOCTOR SERVICE
OF AUSTRALIA

02

03

02 | In the tents guests enjoy luxury that harks back to pioneer times. Even the bed is fit for a king.

In den Zelten herrscht Luxus wie zu Pionierzeiten. Selbst das Bett ist so groß wie für Könige.

03 | The bar is a popular meeting place, and offers great views of the stunning scenery.

Die Bar dient nicht nur als Treff, sondern ist Schaufenster für eine eindrucksvolle Landschaft.

whare kea lodge | wanaka . new zealand

DESIGN: Mayne & Bailieu Architects, Inarc Design Group

Whare Kea Lodge is a luxurious retreat on New Zealand's South Island. Despite the name, which means "house of the Kea parrot" in Maori, the Australian architect John Mayne drew a lot of his inspiration from traditional New Zealand sheep-shearing sheds. The understated, geometric shapes contrast wonderfully with the austere beauty of the New Zealand Alps. It was originally built as a private holiday residence in 1995, which is why it only has six rooms. With its minimalist aesthetic, the interior décor mirrors the appearance of the ensemble as a whole. The lightweight construction, with its glass-paneled walls, ensures that rooms are kept warm, airy and naturally lit. Select antiques and ethnological works of art, as well as carefully coordinated color schemes and natural materials, including untreated wood in the tabletops and floors, complete the picture of this natural refuge. Whare Kea Lodge is a member of Relais & Chateaux. In 2004 it was awarded the prestigious hotel association's environmental award because of its all-embracing commitment to environmental protection. The lodge is ideally situated for heli-skiing tours, walking and fishing.

Whare Kea Lodge, das „Haus des Kea-Papageis", so heißt das luxuriöse Hotel auf der Südinsel Neuseelands in der Sprache der Maoris. Doch der australische Architekt John Mayne hat sich bei der Gestaltung der Anlage eher von den traditionellen neuseeländischen Schafschurhallen inspirieren lassen. Das Understatement der strengen geometrischen Formensprache korrespondiert daher ausgezeichnet mit der herben Schönheit der neuseeländischen Alpenlandschaft. Auch die Innenausstattung der Lodge, 1995 ursprünglich als privates Feriendomizil konzipiert und deshalb mit nur sechs Zimmern ausgestattet, unterstützt mit ihrer minimalistischen Ästhetik den Gesamteindruck des Ensembles. Die transparente Leichtbauweise lässt die Räume je nach Jahreszeit von Licht, Luft und Wärme durchfluten. Ausgesuchte Antiquitäten und Ethnokunst sowie sorgsam abgestimmte Farben und Materialien wie etwa unbehandelte Tischplatten und Holzfußböden runden das Bild dieses Natur-Refugiums ab. Als Mitglied der Hotelvereinigung Relais & Chateaux gewann das Gästehaus im Jahr 2004 den Umweltpreis für sein allumfassendes Engagement im Umweltschutz. Die Lodge dient auch als Ausgangspunkt für Helikopter-Skiing, zum Wandern und Fischen.

02 | 03 When the weather is fine guests love to be outside.

Bei schönem Wetter sind die Gäste gerne draußen.

04 | View from the lodge of Lake Wanaka and the mountains.

Blick von der Lodge auf den Lake Wanaka und die Berge.

02

03 04

yasawa island resort | yasawa . fiji island

DESIGN: Gath Downey

Yasawa Island, 22 kilometers long and a mere 1,000 meters wide, extends like a long, narrow ribbon to the west of the large Fijian islands Vanua Levu and Viti Levu. Yasawa Island Resort, which was founded in 1991 and renovated in 2003, offers splendid isolation, total peace and quiet and an escape from the pressures of everyday life. Baggage is limited to 15 kilograms per person. One of the two small islands at the southern end of Yasawa Island was the location for the movie "The Blue Lagoon". The resort offers 18 exquisite beach villas (bures), each standing alone in a secluded bay of powder-fine sand. Rooms are open-plan and are in a clean, contemporary style with Fijian accents. Diving and snorkeling open up the pristine, multicolored underwater world. The hotel offers trips to the Blue Lagoon caves, rainforest adventure flights, visits to Fijian dance festivals, Aborigine-led birdwatching walks and nature discovery tours to the Great Barrier Reef, which is not far offshore. A waterfall in the resort grounds provides pure, bubbling spring water for the pool and the spa.

Die 22 km lange und nur 1000 Meter breite Yasawa Island erstreckt sich als langes, schmales Band westlich der großen Fijiinseln Vanua Levu und Viti Levu. Hier liegt das 1991 gegründete und 2003 renovierte Yasawa Island Resort. Weitab von Trubel und Termindruck findet man hier eine Stätte ungewöhnlicher Stille und Einsamkeit – in die jedoch kein Gast eingeflogen wird, der mehr als 15 Kilogramm Gepäck mitnehmen möchte. Eine der zwei kleinen Inseln am Südende von Yasawa Island erlangte als Drehort und Namensgeber für den Film „Die blaue Lagune" Weltruhm. Die Anlage besteht aus 18 exquisiten Strandvillen (Bures), jede für sich in einer abgeschlossenen Bucht mit puderfeinem Sand gelegen. Die Räume sind in klarem, modernem Design mit regionalen Akzenten gehalten und gehen offen ineinander über. Beim Tauchen und Schnorcheln kann eine bunte, unberührte Unterwasserwelt erkundet werden. Das Hotel bietet Trips zu den Höhlen der Blauen Lagune, Abenteuerausflüge durch den Regenwald, den Besuch eines Tanzfestes der Einheimischen sowie Vogelkundeführungen durch Aborigines oder Naturerkundungen am nicht weit entfernten Great Barrier Reef vor der Küste. Ein Wasserfall auf dem Gelände des Resorts liefert reines, prickelndes Quellwasser für Pool und den Spa.

01 | Each beach villa has a private beach beneath palm trees.

Jede Strandvilla besitzt einen eigenen Strand unter Palmen.

02 | View of the living and sleeping area: stone floors and a contemporary interior under a wooden roof.

Blick in einen Schlaf- und Wohnraum: Steinfußböden und modernes Interieur unter einem Holzdach.

03 | Bathrooms are simple but functional.

Einfach, aber funktional sind die Bäder gestaltet.

jumeirah bab al shams | dubai . united arab emirates

DESIGN: Keith Gavin, Godwin Austen Johnson, Karen Wilhelmm, Mirage Mille

The contrast could hardly be more pronounced. In Dubai City, the hyper-modern Burj Al Arab hotel is an architectural icon of the 21st century, while the Bab Al Shams resort is reminiscent of ancient Arabian desert settlements—however both establishments are members of Jumeirah, the prestigious luxury hotels group. From the city, it takes just over half an hour by car to reach this desert hotel. It has 105 rooms and ten suites, and its interiors are resplendent with natural stones, dark wooden furniture and oriental glass art. Because of the hotel's two-story construction, rooms either have a terrace with access to the garden, or a spacious balcony. The "Al Forsan" restaurant is located in the middle of the complex. Its terrace provides fantastic views of the garden and the hotel swimming pool. Regular guests tend to head to "Al Hadheerah"—the only authentic open-air restaurant in the region. As well as traditional Arabian dishes, it also features live bands, dancers and henna artists. Attached to the hotel is the Santani Spa. Treatments can be conducted either in private rooms or out in the open air. Soothing massages are a particular specialty.

Kontrastreicher geht es wohl kaum. Während das hypermoderne Hotel Burj Al Arab in Dubai City als Synonym für das 21. Jahrhundert steht, präsentiert sich das Jumeirah Bab Al Shams Resort wie eine alte arabische Wüstensiedlung – beide Häuser gehören aber zur renommierten Jumeirah-Gruppe. In gut einer halben Stunde gelangt man mit dem Pkw von Dubai in das von Wüste umgebene Hotel. 105 Zimmer und zehn Suiten stehen den Gästen zur Verfügung. Das Interieur besteht aus Natursteinen, dunklen Holzmöbeln und orientalischen Glasarbeiten. Da die Räume in doppelstöckigen Gebäuden untergebracht sind, haben die Gäste die Wahl zwischen einer Terrasse mit Gartenzugang oder einem großen Balkon im Obergeschoss. Im Zentrum der Anlage liegt das Restaurant Al Forsan. Von der Terrasse aus hat man einen schönen Blick in den Garten und auf den Swimmingpool des Hotels. Stammgäste zieht es meist aber in das Al Hadheerah Desert Restaurant – es ist das einzige authentische Freiluftlokal in der Gegend. Geboten werden Ethnospeisen, zur Unterhaltung Live-Bands, Tänzerinnen und Henna-Malerinnen. Dem Hotel angegliedert ist der Santani Spa. Alle Behandlungen werden entweder in geschlossenen Räumen oder auf Wunsch unter freiem Himmel durchgeführt. Eine Spezialität sind exotische Massagen.

01 | A shining example of traditional Arab architecture.

Konsequent umgesetzte traditionelle arabische Architektur.

02 | The hotel complex enjoys a secluded desert location.
Die Hotelanlage liegt abgeschieden in der Wüste

03

03 | All houses are elegantly linked with one another.
Alle Häuser sind elegant miteinander verbunden.

04 | Simple furniture embellished by oriental decorations.
Schlichtes Mobiliar ergänzt durch orientalische Elemente.

north island | north island . seychelles

DESIGN: Silvio Rech & Lesley Carstens Architecture and Interior Architecture

Without a doubt, North Island is one of those once-in-a-lifetime experiences that are well worth saving for. Architects and designers Silvio Rech and Lesley Carsten have created a brilliant fusion of ethnic style and meditative purism—natural wood floors, plump upholstery, a sea of plush cushions and contemporary designer furniture. There is a pool hewn into the rock and a minimalist, mirror-like water channel. None of this would have been possible without the German visionary Wolfgang Burre and a group of like-minded people. They bought up the entire island and built eleven guest villas, each approximately 450 square meters. North Island is around 15 minutes from Mahé by helicopter and at a distance of a few hundred meters the island appears almost uninhabited. It is Wolfgang Burre's intention to keep it that way—unspoilt and rich in plant and animal life. He even decided against a jetty, maintaining it would spoil the view and be just too convenient. Guests going on a trip by boat have to wade the last few meters through emerald-green waters on soft, velvety sand, with relaxation mode kicking in, if it hasn't done so already.

Zweifellos, diese Adresse zählt zu den „Einmal-im-Leben-Geschenken", für die es sich lohnt zu sparen. Virtuos hat es das Architekten- und Designerpaar Silvio Rech und Lesley Carsten verstanden, urige Gemütlichkeit und meditativen Purismus zu kombinieren. Hier ein Boden mit sägerauen Dielen, dazwischen dicke Polster und ein Meer aus plüschigen Kissen, darauf modernes Architekten-Mobiliar. Hier ein in den Fels gehauener Pool, dort ein minimalistischer, spiegelglatter Wasserkanal. Ermöglicht hat dies eine von Visionen beseelte Eignergruppe um den Deutschen Wolfgang Burre. Sie kauften die gesamte Insel rund 15 Helikopterminuten entfernt von Mahé und statteten sie mit elf Gästevillen aus, von denen jede 450 Quadratmetern groß ist. Bei so dünner Population wirkt die Insel aus ein paar hundert Metern Entfernung fast unbewohnt. Ganz im Sinne Wolfgang Burres, der die Ursprünglichkeit der Insel mit all ihren Pflanzen- und Tierarten erhalten möchte. Sogar auf einen Bootsanlegesteg hat er verzichtet. „Stört die Optik und macht bequem", so Burre. Wer mit dem Boot Ausflüge macht, darf deshalb die letzten paar Meter durch das smaragdgrüne Wasser auf weichem Sand waten. Spätestens dabei wird die innere Uhr auf Entspannung geschaltet.

01 | The piazza right on East Beach with the bar and lounge behind.

Die Piazza direkt am East Beach, dahinter anschließend Bar und Lounge.

02 | A luxurious bathroom adjoins each bedroom.

Ein großzügig angelegtes Badezimmer, das jedem Schlafbereich angeschlossen ist.

02

03 | Breakfast and living area in one of the island's eleven villas.

Frühstücks- und Wohnbereich in einer der elf Villen der Insel.

04 | View of one of the North Island villas.

Blick auf eine der North Island Villen.

alfajiri villas | diani beach . kenya

DESIGN: Marika Molinaro

Italian couple Fabrizio and Marika Molinaro have fulfilled their dream of owning a guest house on the Indian Ocean—Alfajiri is right on secluded Diani Beach, around an hour from Mombasa. Marika Molinaro, an interior designer, furnished the villas herself, with great attention to detail. She made all furniture herself. Walls are hung with numerous pictures and wood carvings brought back by husband Fabrizio, a former medical doctor, from extensive tours of Africa and the Far East. There is a cliff villa, a garden villa and a beach villa, each to accommodate eight. The layout ensures each party their own private space, and the design provides plenty of air circulation, enabling guests to sleep with the windows open. Fabrizio and Monika Molinaro have evidently struck the right note with their discerning clientele. Alfajiri is a fascinating mix of luxurious furnishings, valuable artifacts from various parts of the world and makuti roofs woven from palm straw. Children are very welcome at Alfajiri. Two nannies, both of whom speak English, are available to look after your children all day.

Direkt am abgeschiedenen Diani Beach, etwa eine Stunde von Mombasa entfernt, hat sich das italienische Ehepaar Molinari ihren Traum vom eigenen Gästehaus am Indischen Ozean erfüllt. Marika Molinaro ist Innenausstatterin und hat bei der Einrichtung ihrer Alfajiri Villen auf jedes Detail geachtet. Die Möbel hat sie alle selbst gefertigt. An den Wänden befinden sich zahlreiche Bilder und Holzschnitzereien, die ihr Ehemann Fabricio, ein ehemaliger Arzt, von seinen ausgiebigen Reisen durch Afrika und dem Fernen Osten mitgebracht hat. Es gibt eine Cliff, Garden und Beach Villa, die jeweils Platz für acht Gäste bieten. Sie sind so angelegt, dass die jeweiligen Bewohner stets unter sich bleiben. Die Bauweise ermöglicht eine Luftzirkulation, die es erlaubt, bei offenem Fenster zu schlafen. Mit ihrem Ambiente, einer Mischung aus höchstem Komfort, hochwertiger Kunst aus verschiedenen Teilen der Welt und den aus Palmstroh geflochtenen Makuti-Dächern, treffen die Molinaris offensichtlich genau den Geschmack ihrer zahlungskräftigen Gäste. Kinder sind in Alfajiri übrigens gern gesehen. Zwei Englisch sprechende Nannys kümmern sich auf Wunsch auch den ganzen Tag um den Nachwuchs.

01 | Fabrizio and Monika Molinaro's villas are on secluded Diani Beach.

Die Häuser der Molinaros liegen am abgeschiedenen Diani Beach.

02 | 03 | 04 Artifacts from Africa and Asia adorn the villas.

Kunstwerke aus Afrika und Asien schmücken die Villen.

bateleur camp at kichwa tembo | kichwa tembo . kenya

DESIGN: Nick Plewman, Chris Browne

Kichwa Tembo Lodge in the west of the Masai Mara Park is particularly suitable for safari holidaymakers wishing to discover Kenya's wildlife well away from the main tourist centers. Kichwa Tembo means "head of the elephant"—a reference to the many pachyderms that splash about at the reserve's watering holes. The Masai Mara Park is best known for its enormous herds of wildebeest and zebra. It is also home to vast numbers of rhinos, lions, giraffes and over 400 species of birds. The camp's luxurious tents are surrounded by trees and decorated in the style of the 1920's, recalling the movie "Out of Africa", whose famous final scene, the funeral of safari hunter Denys Finch (Robert Redford), was shot at the exact spot where the lodge now stands. Each tent has a private veranda with views of the Masai Mara savanna or the Sabaringo river. If desired, dinner can be served by a personal butler. The camp offers excursions to Maasai villages and walks along the Mara river or the Rift Valley, where there are many lava fields, volcanoes and hot springs.

Die im Westen des Massai-Mara-Parks gelegene Kichwa Tembo Lodge eignet sich vor allem für Safari-Urlauber, die fernab der Touristenzentren die Tierwelt Kenias kennen lernen möchten. Der Name der Lodge heißt übersetzt soviel wie „Kopf des Elefanten" – ein Hinweis auf die vielen Dickhäuter, die sich an den Wasserstellen des Reservats tummeln. Bekannt ist der Massai Mara Park jedoch vor allem als Wandergebiet riesiger Gnu- und Zebraherden. Auch zahlreiche Nashörner, Löwen, Giraffen und mehr als 400 Vogelarten sind dort zu Hause. Die von Bäumen umgebenen Luxuszelte des Camps sind im Stil der 20er Jahre errichtet und erinnern an den Film „Jenseits von Afrika". Die berühmte letzte Szene des Hollywood-Streifens, die Beerdigung des Safari-Jägers Denys Finch (Robert Redford), wurde genau an dem Ort gedreht, wo sich heute die Lodge befindet. Jedes Zelt verfügt über eine eigene Veranda mit Blick auf die Massai Mara Steppe oder den Sabaringo Fluss. Auf Wunsch serviert der persönliche Butler dort auch das Abendessen. Vom Camp aus bieten sich Ausflüge zu Massai-Siedlungen sowie Wanderungen entlang des Mara Rivers oder des Rift Valleys an. Dort befinden sich zahlreiche Lavafelder, Vulkane und heiße Quellen.

02 | Many animals can be observed from the camp.

Vom Camp aus lassen sich zahlreiche Tiere beobachten.

03 | The lodge is ideal for safari holidaymakers.

Die Lodge ist ideal für Safari-Urlauber.

03

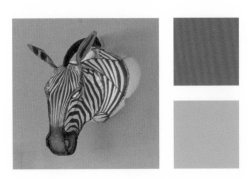

hatari lodge | mount meru . tanzania

DESIGN: Jörg & Marlies Gabriel with Remy Macha

Opened in 2004, Hatari Lodge is on the northern edge of the Arusha National Park. It is situated at an altitude of 1,500 meters at the foot of Mount Kilimanjaro, Africa's highest mountain (5,892 meters). The lodge takes its name from the Hollywood movie "Hatari", which was filmed here. The old houses and farm—home to actor Hardy Krüger for 17 years—are now the centerpiece of the lodge. Its terraces offer sweeping views of wildlife-rich savanna clearings, magical rainforests and mountain peaks sometimes topped with snow—the perfect movie backdrop dominated by Mount Kilimanjaro and its neighbor Mount Meru, an extinct volcano. There are nine well-appointed rooms furnished in 60's and 70's style, each with an open fireplace, a spacious bathroom and a private veranda. From the lodge terrace a walkway leads to the Momella clearing, where buffalo graze daily, warthogs rummage for tubers and giraffes venture right to the doorstep. Africa in close-up. The oldest of the farm buildings serves as the central communal area, a large lounge with an open fireplace where the Hatari hosts pass on insider tips and information about the area and its people. There is also an atmospheric bar and a small library.

In 1500 Metern Höhe am Fuße des Kilimanjaro – dem mit 5892 Metern höchsten Berg Afrikas – liegt am Nordrand des Arusha Nationalparks die 2004 eröffnete Hatari Lodge. Die alten Wohnhäuser neben den Farmgebäuden von Hardy Krüger, der hier 17 Jahre lebte, bilden das Herzstück der Lodge. Der gleichnamige Hollywoodfilm "Hatari" wurde an diesem Ort gedreht. Von den Terrassen des Anwesens eröffnet sich der Blick auf tierreiche Savannenlichtungen, märchenhafte Regenwälder und von Zeit zu Zeit schneebedeckte Gipfel. Die perfekte Filmkulisse wird durch den Kilimanjaro dominiert, gleich im Anschluss der mittlerweile erloschene Vulkanberg Mount Meru. Insgesamt neun komfortable Zimmer, alle von der Besitzerin im Stil der 60er und 70er eingerichtet, stehen dem Gast zur Verfügung. Jedes Zimmer besitzt einen Kamin, ein großzügiges Bad und eine eigene Veranda. Von der Lodge-Terrasse gelangt man über einen Steg zur Momella-Lichtung, wo täglich Büffel weiden, Warzenschweine nach Knollen wühlen und sich zahlreiche Giraffen bis teilweise vor die Türschwellen der Lodge heranwagen. Dort erlebt man Afrika hautnah. Das älteste Farmhaus bildet den zentralen Aufenthaltsbereich. Am Kamin informieren die Gastgeber dort über Land und Leute und geben auch schon mal Insidertipps preis. Ein weiterer Teil der großen Lounge ist eine stilvolle Bar und eine kleine Bibliothek.

02

02 | 03 | 04 Lounge and dining room furnished in hip, retro 60's style.

Ein im hippen Retrostil der 1960er Jahre eingerichteter Wohn- und Essraum.

ngorongoro crater lodge | ngorongoro crater . tanzania

DESIGN: Silvio Rech & Lesley Carstens Architecture and Interior Architecture

Ngorongoro Crater Lodge is on the north-west rim of the Ngorongoro volcanic crater, which was formed millions of years ago. Inspired by the layout and appearance of a Maasai village, the lodge comprises three independent, discreet, luxury camps offering a total of 30 suites. All three exclusive camps have guest areas and terraces with vast glazed expanses affording spectacular views of the Ngorongoro Crater and the surrounding Tanzanian countryside. The scene becomes even more stunning when zebra and other wild animals move into view and also at night when huge fire bowls light up the dining room walkways. Warm shades of ruby, silver and gold bathe the rooms in a pleasing light, and chandeliers, wall mirrors, velvet drapes and wood paneling from Zanzibar underline the muted, sophisticated ambience of Ngorongoro Crater Lodge. The very refined atmosphere is combined with local materials, such as banana-leaf ceilings and grass roofs. The lodge sources many goods direct from the Maasai community. Approximately 42,000 Maasai people live in the Ngorongoro Conservation Area, grazing their herds in the unspoilt landscape and living in peaceful harmony with nature. Visits to the Maasai villages are highly recommended.

Am nordwestlichen Rand des Vulkankraters Ngorongoro, der vor Jahrmillionen in sich zusammenfiel, befindet sich die Ngorongoro Crater Lodge. Angelehnt an die Struktur und das Erscheinungsbild eines Dorfes der Massai bilden drei diskrete und luxuriöse Camps mit insgesamt 30 Suiten die Lodge. Diese drei exklusiven Camps sind unabhängig voneinander. Ihre jeweiligen Gemeinschaftsräume und -terrassen geben durch große verglaste Flächen den Blick auf den Ngorongoro Krater und die umliegende Landschaft Tanzanias frei. Die Kulisse wird noch spektakulärer, wenn Zebras und andere wild lebende Tiere auf der Bildfläche erscheinen oder die Aufgänge der Speiseräume bei Nacht durch riesige Feuerschalen erleuchtet werden. Warme Farbtöne aus Silber, Gold und Rubinrot tauchen die Räume in ein angenehmes Licht. Kronleuchter, Spiegel an den Wänden, Samtdeckenüberwürfe und Holzwandvertäfelungen aus Sansibar unterstreichen die gedämpfte, noble Stimmung der Ngorongoro Crater Lodge. Das sehr edel gehaltene Ambiente wird mit Materialien aus der Gegend, wie Decken aus Bananenblättern und Grasdächern kombiniert. Die Lodge bezieht viele Güter direkt von der Gemeinschaft der Massai, die im Ngorongoro Schutzgebiet mit circa 42.000 Menschen leben. In dieser ursprünglichen Landschaft grasen ihre Tierherden und sie leben in friedlicher Koexistenz mit der Natur. Besuche in die Dörfer der Massai sind sehr zu empfehlen.

02 | 03 | 04 | 05 Luxurious rooms, original accessories and great attention to detail.

Mit viel Liebe zum Detail und originalen Accessoires verwöhnen die Zimmer.

vumbura plains | okavango delta . botswana

DESIGN: Silvio Rech & Lesley Carstens Architecture and Interior Architecture

Long before safaris and Land Rovers existed, Botswana's bushmen used to bury the game they had hunted down to protect it from predatory animals, then on the way back to their village they would pull the meat back out of the ground. In their language "vumbura", means to pull, and it is a little known fact that Vumbura Plains (pronounced Voombera) in the extreme north of Botswana bordering on the Moremi Game Reserve is named after this long-forgotten custom. Nowadays hunting is strictly prohibited in the Okavanga Delta and antelopes, lions, buffalo and elephants are protected by law. The wild animals of the savannah live in harmony with humans and can be observed from a distance of just a few meters. The two Vumbura Camps are luxurious bases for probably the most impressive photo safaris in Botswana. South African husband-and-wife architects Silvio Rech and Lesley Carstens have achieved a virtually perfect blend of unspoilt wilderness with purist luxury. Each of the seven villas is built on a wooden platform only linked to the main building by raised walkways, guaranteeing absolute privacy for guests. All have a private terrace, a plunge pool and an open-air shower, but the main attraction is the panoramic view of the plains, with no window panes to separate you from the natural world. In the evenings guests meet by the campfire to sit in comfort and watch the sun go down and wait for the stars to appear.

Lange bevor es Safaris und Landrover gab, haben Botswanas Buschmänner auf Jagdzügen ihr erlegtes Wild im Boden vergraben, um ihre Beute vor Raubtieren zu schützen. Auf dem Rückweg in ihr Dorf zogen sie das Fleisch wieder aus der Erde; in ihrer Sprache „vumbura". Nur wenige wissen, dass der heute längst in Vergessenheit geratene Brauch den Vumbura Plains (ausgesprochen Voombera) im äußersten Norden Botswanas, angrenzend an das Moremi Game Reservat seinen Namen gab. Heute herrscht im Okavango Delta ein striktes Jagdverbot. Antilopen, Löwen, Büffel und Elefanten sind streng geschützt. Die wilden Tiere der Savanne leben im Einklang mit den Menschen und lassen sich aus wenigen Metern Entfernung beobachten. Luxuriöser Ausgangspunkt für die wohl beeindruckendsten Fotosafaris in Botswana sind die beiden Vumbura Camps. Das südafrikanische Architekten-Ehepaar Silvio Rech und Lesley Carstens hat hier eine nahezu perfekte Mischung aus unberührter Wildnis und puristischem Luxus geschaffen. Die jeweils sieben Villen stehen auf Holzplattformen und sind nur durch Stege mit dem Hauptgebäude verbunden. Die Unterkünfte bieten somit Privatsphäre pur. Jede Unterkunft hat eine eigene Terrasse, einen Erfrischungspool und eine Freiluftdusche. Ins Schwärmen kommen die Gäste aber vor allem beim Panoramablick auf die Savanne. Denn kein Fensterglas trennt die Gäste von der Natur. Und am Abend trifft man sich bei Sonnenuntergang am lauschigen Feuerplatz und erwartet auf weichen Kissen den Sternenhimmel.

01 | Villa 1 in North Vumbura Camp overlooks a water hole visited by herds of elephants.

Villa 1 im North Camp bietet den Blick auf ein Wasserloch, das von Elefantenherden besucht wird.

02 | One of the few wilderness areas that has recovered from the ravages of the safari era.

Eine der wenigen Gegenden, wo sich die Wildnis von den Sünden der Safari-Ära erholt hat.

04

03 | 04 Living spaces and nature merge.

Wohnräume und Natur verschmelzen.

benguerra lodge | benguerra island . mozambique
DESIGN: Trevor Landrey

The Bazaruto Archipelago was once part of the Mozambique mainland, but it has progressively sunk, leaving its highest points as a chain of islands—five unique eco systems forming the Bazaruto National Park and now lapped by the bio-diverse waters of the Indian Ocean. The park is one of the last remaining habitats for the legendary dugong, a rare type of sea cow. Benguerra Island (55 square kilometers) is the second largest of the islands. Benguerra Lodge enjoys a protected south-west setting in the heart of acacia and mahogany forests. It offers eleven chalets and three villas, all within 20 meters of the beach. Straw roofs, glassless windows with wooden blinds, rustic ethnic furniture and wall hangings create an atmosphere that is half safari tented camp, half turn-of-the-century colonial villa. Benguerra Island is best known for its pristine white beaches, but you don't need to be a nature aficionado to be impressed by its mangrove and swamp forests, unspoilt coral reefs and crocodile-rich freshwater lakes—habitats for a wealth of flora and fauna and legacies of when the island was part of the mainland. Benguerra Lodge is a member of the Khani Kwedo (Our Home) project, which was set up to preserve the island's unspoilt environment.

Einst gehörte das Bazaruto Archipel zum Festland Mozambiques, durch allmähliches Absinken von Landmassen verwandelten sich die höchsten Punkte zur Inselkette. Fünf einzigartige Ökosysteme, die den Bazaruto Nationalpark ausmachen, werden seither von den artenreichen Wassern des Indischen Ozeans umspült. Hier finden die legendären Dugongs – die einzigen lebenden Vertreter der Gabelschwanzseekühe – einen ihrer letzten Rückzugsorte. Benguerra Island ist mit seinen 55 Quadratkilometern die zweitgrößte der Inseln. In geschützter südwest Lage liegen die elf Häuschen und die drei Villen der Benguerra Lodge inmitten von Akazien- und Mahagoniwäldern, alle nicht weiter als 20 Meter vom Strand entfernt. Strohdächer, Fenster ohne Glas nur mit Holzjalousien, rustikale Ethno-Möbel und Wandteppiche vermitteln den Flair einer Mischung aus Safarizeltlager und Kolonialvilla der Jahrhundertwende. Benguerra Island ist zwar vor allem bekannt für ihre weißen Traumstände, aber nicht nur ausgesprochene Naturliebhaber sind beeindruckt von Mangroven- und Moorwäldern, unberührten Korallenriffen und den krokodilreichen Süßwasserseen, die an die Festlandzeit der Insel erinnern und die Grundlage für die reiche Flora und Fauna bilden. Mit dem Ziel die Ursprünglichkeit der Insel zu erhalten, wurde das Projekt Khani Kwedi (unsere Heimat), an dem auch Benguerra Lodge beteiligt ist, gegründet.

01 | The early morning light of the tropics and the distant calls of exotic birds, of which there are over 125 species.

Morgendliches Tropenlicht und aus der Ferne ertönen exotische Laute einiger Vertreter der über 125 Vogelarten.

02 | The lodge offers western-style luxury in the heart of nature for only 30 people at a time.

Nicht mehr als 30 Leute gleichzeitig können den Luxus westlicher Standards in unberührter Natur beanspruchen.

03 | The interior design features the craftsmanship of the island's inhabitants.

Die Handwerkskunst der Inselbewohner bestimmt das Design des Interieurs.

mowani mountain camp | damaraland . namibia
DESIGN: Andre Louw, Klaus Brandt

Mountainous Damaraland extends south-west of the Etosha Pan in north-western Namibia. It is home to the Damara and the Bushmen, Namibia's earliest inhabitants, whose forefathers lived here some 10,000 years ago. They are immortalized by cave engravings near Twyfelfontein, today one of the most extensive archaeological finds of its kind in the world. This ancient landscape is also the setting for Mowani. At first glance there are no signs of civilization: the camp is perfectly camouflaged within the landscape. A second glance reveals domed, thatched roofs among enormous red boulders. Twelve luxury tents with private terrace are built on stilts, well spaced between giant rock formations that seem to absorb any sound. At night candlelight is the only illumination, and only where needed. Natural pathways lead to the dining room, lounge and rock pool. Guests can enjoy the African sun on the pool deck or beneath the thatched sunshades.

Das bergige Damaraland erstreckt sich im Nordwesten Namibias süd-westlich der Etosha Pfanne. Es ist die Heimat der Damara und Bushmen – der ältesten Einwohner Namibias, deren Vorfahren schon vor etwa zehntausend Jahren hier lebten und sich mit Gravuren auf Felswände rund um Twyfelfontein verewigten – heute eine der weltweit umfang-reichsten Fundstätten dieser Art. In dieser archaischen Landschaft liegt Mowani. Beim ersten Hinsehen sind keine Spuren von Zivilisation zu erkennen. Das Camp ist in der Landschaft perfekt getarnt. Erst auf den zweiten Blick entdeckt man die Kuppeln reetgedeckter Dächer zwischen den enormen rötlichen Findlingen. Zwölf auf Stelzen gebaute Zeltun-terkünfte mit Terrasse liegen weitläufig eingebettet zwischen riesigen Steinformationen, die jegliches Geräusch zu schlucken scheinen. Nachts sind sie nur mit Kerzenlicht an den nötigsten Stellen beleuchtet. Naturbe-lassene Wege führen zum Esszimmer, zur Lounge und weiter zum Felsen-pool. Auf der daneben angelegten Terrasse oder unter reetgedeckten Sonnendächern kann man tagsüber die afrikanische Sonne pur genießen.

01 | The reception huts resemble an African village set among gigantic granite marbles.

Die Hütten der Rezeption erscheinen wie ein afrikanisches Dorf inmitten gigantischer Granitmurmeln.

02

03 04

05

02 | View of the dry Aba Huab riverbed from the bedroom of the luxury suite.

Blick vom Schlafraum der Luxury Suite auf das ausgetrocknete Aba Huab Flussbett.

03 | Traditional African artifacts add a final flourish.

Traditionelle afrikanische Kunstobjekte ergänzen die Einrichtung.

04 | From the pool guests can look out on Damaraland's endless expanses.

Vom Pool aus kann man die endlose Weite des Damaralands genießen.

05 | The bathtub, on a wooden platform, offers stunning views.

Die auf der Holzplattform thronende Wanne lädt zum Eintauchen in die Natur ein.

onguma tented camp | etosha national park . namibia
DESIGN: Andre Louw, Johann Slee

Onguma Safari Camp is on the eastern side of the Etosha National Park in northern Namibia, the largest of its kind in the country. It is a privileged location for close-up observation of African wildlife on the banks of watering holes. The Herero word Onguma means "the place you don't want to leave", a sentiment embodied by seven tents in the more exclusive part of the camp, which are equipped with every conceivable luxury. The U-shape design of the safari accommodation provides both privacy and open views, including plenty of opportunity for bird spotting—there are some 300 local species. Each tent has an indoor and an outdoor shower, a bathtub, a separate WC and 2 washbasins. There is also a shared pool. Carefully chosen natural materials—linen and wood, for example—are used in the décor, but guests can still enjoy creature comforts like fans, lighting and large, comfortable beds, even in the midst of the African bush. Safaris and excursions are offered from the camp.

Das Onguma Safari Camp liegt auf der östlichen Seite des Etosha National Parks im Norden Namibias. Dieser ist der größte seiner Art in dem Land. Ein einzigartiger Ort, um an den Ufern der Wasserstellen die wilde Tierwelt Afrikas hautnah beobachten zu können. In dieser Umgebung liegt das Onguma Camp, das in der Sprache der Hereros soviel bedeutet wie „der Platz, den Du nicht verlassen willst". Um den Gästen dieses Gefühl zu vermitteln, wurden im exklusiveren Teil des Camps sieben Zelte mit allem erdenklichen Komfort ausgestattet. Die U-förmige Anordnung der Safariunterkünfte gewährt einerseits Privatsphäre, andererseits bleibt der Blick in die Umgebung frei. So hat man unter anderem die Chance einige der insgesamt rund 300 Vogelarten der Gegend zu erspähen. Jedes Zelt ist mit Duschen im Innen- und Außenbereich, Badewanne, abgetrenntem WC und 2 Waschbecken ausgestattet. Ein gemeinsamer Pool steht allen Gästen zur Verfügung. Mit großer Sorgfalt wurden natürliche Materialien für die Ausstattung verwendet, wie Leinen, Holz, und trotzdem muss der Gast auch im so genannten Busch nicht auf modernen Komfort, wie Ventilatoren, Licht und bequeme, große Betten verzichten. Vom Camp aus werden Safaris und Ausflüge angeboten.

02 | A modern interpretation of an old zinc bathtub.

Eine moderne Interpretation einer alten Zinkbadewanne.

03 | The outdoor pool.

Der Pool im Außenbereich.

04 | Light, natural colors in the safari tent.

Helle, natürliche Farben im Safari Zelt.

05 | Small details create the perfect ensemble.

Viele Details summieren sich zu einem perfekten Ensemble.

03
04 05

grootbos | hermanus-gansbaai . south africa

DESIGN: Vaughan Russlle, Eloise Collocott-Russlle, Dorothé Lutzeyer

Not far from the Cape of Good Hope is the Grootbos Private Nature Reserve, a haven of peace and relaxation for nature lovers. True to the Grootbos Foundation's commitment to nature conservation, there are no hordes of holidaymakers in this small paradise, just low-impact tourism. The same concept is also reflected in the design and architecture of the original, country-house-style Garden Lodge and the contemporary-style Forest Lodge, which was added only two years ago. There are 23 separate suites accessed via winding pathways through the fynbos park. Their interior decor is strikingly plain, playfully contrasting nature and civilization. The terraces look out onto the lush garden and the fynbos park, which extends to the dunes and cliffs at Walker Bay. It all seems virtually untouched, with penguins and seals playing about uninhibited in the water. 30 meters offshore it is even possible to see right whales swimming into this protected bay. While the adults relax, swim or take a walk along the long beaches, children can enjoy a short adventure boat ride to the seal and whale colonies.

Unweit des Kap der guten Hoffnung finden Naturliebhaber im Grootbos Private Nature Reserve Ruhe und Entspannung. Eingebettet in das Naturschutz-Konzept der Grootbos Foundation gibt es in diesem kleinen Paradies keine Urlauber-Scharen, sondern nur sanften Tourismus. Dazu passt auch die Gestaltung und Philosophie der ursprünglich, im Landhausstil erbauten Garden Lodge und der erst vor zwei Jahren in zeitgenössischer Architektur hinzugefügten Forest Lodge. Zur Lodge gehören 23 separate Suiten, die über verschlungene Wege im Fynbos Park zu erreichen sind. Im spielerischen Kontrast zwischen Zivilisation und Natur wurden die Räume in einem betont sachlichen Stil eingerichtet. Die Terrassen bieten einen Blick auf den üppig bewachsenen Garten und in die Landschaft des Fynbos Parks. Dessen Vegetation reicht bis zu den Dünen und Klippen der Walker Bay. Alles wirkt beinahe unberührt, denn im Wasser tummeln sich ohne Scheu Pinguine und Robben. 30 Meter vom Ufer entfernt sieht man sogar Glattwale, die in diese geschützte Bucht kommen. Während sich die Erwachsenen an den langen Stränden beim Schwimmen oder bei Spaziergängen erholen, können die Kinder an kleinen Abenteuer-Bootsfahrten zu den Revieren der Robben und Wale teilnehmen.

01 | Natural stone and wood are the main materials at the lodge.

Natursteine und Holz sind die am meisten verwendeten
Materialien der Lodge.

02

02 | Guaranteed sun and crystal-clear water.

Ein Platz mit Sonnengarantie und glasklarem Wasser.

03 | The bar and lounge are in the main Grootbos Lodge building.

Im Haupthaus der Grootbos Lodge befinden sich Bar und Lounge.

03

04 | Walker Bay is very close to the hotel.

Die Walker Bay liegt in unmittelbarer Nähe zum Hotel.

05 | Bedrooms have an innovative lighting design.

Im Schlafraum wurde ein originelles Lichtkonzept verwirklicht.

04

singita sweni lodge | kruger national park . south africa
DESIGN: Andrew Makin, Design Workshop; Boyd Ferguson, Cecile and Boyd

In the South African Shangaan language, Singita means "place of miracles"—a perfect description of this location. Singita Sweni Lodge is the smallest and most tucked-away of the Singita lodges, but is no less exclusive for that. It is set in dense forest in the south-east of South Africa's famous Kruger Park. Its charm lies in its seclusion, its position right on the banks of the Sweni river (from which it takes its name) and its accommodation which is hidden away in the dappled shade of the trees. The suites, six in total, are built on stilts and have a roof deck of dark wood. Each suite is a study in contrasts—a mix of traditional craft items, ceramic bowls for instance, and contemporary furniture. Fresh, light colors also contrast with earthy, dark shades of brown. Guests can take safaris from the lodge and, with a little luck, see the "big five"—elephant, rhino, buffalo, lion and leopard. As the proprietors rightly claim, "Sweni is a place that leaves a lasting impression on the spirit".

Singita heißt „Platz der Wunder" und kommt aus dem südafrikanischen Shangaan – tatsächlich könnte nichts diesen Platz besser umschreiben. Im südöstlichen Teil des berühmten Krüger Parks in Südafrika, umschlossen von dicht gewachsenem Wald befindet sich die Singita Sweni Lodge, die kleinste und zurückgezogen liegendste der Lodgen, deren Größe aber nichts über ihre Exklusivität verrät. Sie besticht durch ihre Zurückgezogenheit. Die Lage direkt am Flussufer des Sweni Rivers, der gleichzeitig Namensgeber der Lodge ist, macht den Reiz ebenso aus, wie das Versteckspiel der Unterkünfte unter schattigen Bäumen. Die Hütten, insgesamt sechs an der Zahl, sind auf einer Pfahlbautenkonstruktion errichtet, die Dachterrasse ist aus dunklem Holz erbaut. Tritt man in eines der Häuschen ein, so eröffnet sich ein Raum, der vom Kontrast lebt. Alte volkstümliche Handwerkskunst, wie Keramikschalen werden mit modernen Möbelstücken kombiniert. Helle frische sowie dunkle erdige Brauntöne nehmen am Kontrastspiel teil. Von hier aus kann man Safaris ins Umland starten und mit ein wenig Glück auch die Big Five (Elefanten, Nashorn, Büffel, Löwe, Leopard) sehen. „Sweni ist ein Ort der nachhaltig den Geist beeinflusst", damit werben die Gastgeber zu Recht.

01 | Glimpse inside one of the six suites.
Blick in eines der insgesamt sechs Häuschen.

03

02 | 03 Interiors are a charming mix of indigenous crafts and contemporary luxury.

Den Reiz des Interieurs macht die Kombination aus heimischer Handwerkskunst und modernem Komfort aus.

tsala treetop lodge | plettenberg . south africa
DESIGN: Bruce Stafford & Hunter family

Tsala Treetop Lodge, situated between the Tsitsikamma mountains and the Indian Ocean, makes it possible to combine luxury with Africa at its most unspoilt. It offers ten well-appointed suites built on tall stilts and linked to the main building and restaurant via a network of wooden walkways. The lodge is set beneath a canopy of ancient treetops in virgin forest. The design—both interior and exterior—is a stylish blend of stone, wood, glass and traditional African furniture. All suites are furnished with textiles and carvings by South African artists and have a private pool and sundeck. Guests often find themselves bathing in the company of exotic birds. The lodge covers 80 hectares in total, its elevated position affording fabulous views of the mountain valleys nearby. The layout of the suites guarantees privacy and gives each party their own small patch of forest. In the evenings guests often gather in the restaurant to enjoy exquisite, light cuisine and some of the country's finest red wines—the perfect end to a long day in the South African forest.

Gäste, die einen Aufenthalt in dieser Lodge genießen wollen, erwartet eine Kombination aus luxuriösem Wohnen und dem ursprünglichem Afrika. Auf hohen Pfählen gebaut, verbindet ein Netz von Holzstegen zehn komfortable Suiten mit dem Haupthaus, in dem sich auch das Restaurant befindet. Die gesamte Lodge – sie liegt zwischen den Tsitsikamma Bergen und dem Indischen Ozean – schmiegt sich unter die Wipfel alter Urwaldriesen. Stein, Holz, Glas und traditionell afrikanische Möbel wurden für die Innen- und Außengestaltung stilvoll kombiniert. Alle Cottages sind mit Textilien und Schnitzereien südafrikanischer Künstler ausgestaltet und besitzen zudem je einen eigenen Pool und ein Sonnendeck. Nicht selten kommen exotische Vögel angeflogen und leisten den Badenden dann Gesellschaft. Aus der luftigen Perspektive lassen sich aber auch wunderbar die benachbarten Bergtäler bestaunen. Insgesamt 80 Hektar groß ist das gesamte Anwesen. Die Cottages wurden so angelegt, dass die Privatsphäre gewahrt bleibt und jeder Gast sein eigenes kleines „Urwaldreich" bewohnt. Ein Zusammentreffen findet dann häufig gegen Abend im Restaurant statt. Bei besten Rotweinen aus dem Lande und feinen leichten Gerichten enden hier lange Tage in der Natur Südafrikas.

01 | Tsala Treetop Lodge suites are surrounded by ancient trees.

Inmitten uralter Bäume befinden sich die Cottages der Tsala Treetop Lodge.

02

03

02 | Luxury in the heart of nature—comfortable beds, contemporary lighting.

Komfort inmitten der Natur: Luxuriöse Betten, moderne Raumbeleuchtung.

03 | A small woodstove provides warmth in the evenings.

Ein kleiner Holzofen bringt am Abend Wärme in das Cottage.

04 | It fills the room and offers outdoor views—the bathtub in one of the suites.

Raumfüllend und mit Blick nach draußen: die Badewanne in einer Gästesuite.

hotel index

hotel index

Country / Location		Address	Information	Architecture & Design	Page
Belize	San Ignacio	Blancaneaux Mountain Pine Ridge Forest Reserve Belize www.blancaneaux.com	opened 1993 7 villas and 10 cabanas, restaurant and bar, riverside spa, organic garden, located outside the town of San Ignacio in the Mountain Pine Ridge Forest Reserve, 2 hours from Miami by air.	Manolo Mestre	32
Chile	Torres del Paine	Explora en Patagonia Torres del Paine National Park Chile www.explora.com	opened 1993 50 rooms, restaurant, bar and library, indoor pool, jacuzzi, gym and massage, private moorings on the lake, located in the Torres del Paine National Park.	Germán del Sol	36
Chile	Puerto Natales	Remota Puerto Natales Patagonia Chile www.remota.cl	opened 2005 72 rooms housed in 2 buildings, winter garden, big music room, 5 living rooms, restaurant, bar, indoor heated pool, 2 saunas, 2 open air Jacuzzis, located at Puerto Natales fishing port, 250 km or two and a half hours drive from Punta Arenas Airport, Chile's most southern city, airport transport service.	Germán del Sol	40
Peru	Tambopata	Reserva Amazónica Lodge www.reserva-amazonica.info	opened 1975 30 cabanas and 3 suites pavilion housing dining room, bar and main lounge, located in the Amazon Rain Forest in a part of a private eco- logical reserve adjacent to the Tambopata National Park, flights from Puerto Maldonado, pick up by bus at the airport to the river port, 1 hour canoe ride downriver from Puerto Maldonado to the lodge.	Denise Guislain	46
France	Lagarde	Castelnau des Fieumarcon Lagarde 32700 Lectoure France www.lagarde.org	opened 2002 medieval village comprising 17 stone houses with 27 bedrooms and suites able to accommodate up to 60 people, restaurant, reception rooms, located between Lectoure and Condom, close to Toulous International Airport.	Frédéric Coustols	50

hotel index

hotel index

Country / Location		Address	Information	Architecture & Design	Page
Australia	North Queensland	Voyages Coconut Beach Rainforest Lodge Cape Tripulation North Queensland, Australia www.voyages.com.au	opened 1990 66 rooms with private rainforest views, private bathroom, ceiling fans, restaurant and bar, located between the Great Barrier Reef and the Daintree National Park, 140 km north of Cairns, a 2 hours and 30 minutes drive by car.	Watermark	76
Australia	North Queensland	Daintree Eco Lodge & Spa 20 Daintree Road 4873 Daintree, Queensland Australia www.daintree-ecolodge.com.au	reopened 1993 15 rainforest villas, gourmet restaurant, dayspa, pristine natural spring wather bath, in the middle of Daintree National Park, 1 hours and 30 minutes from Cairns.	Cathy and Terry Maloney	80
Australia	Wilson Island	Voyages Wilson Island The Great Barrier Reef Queensland Australia www.voyages.com.au	opened 2002 6 permanent tents for a maximum of 12 guests, open kitchen and lounge, located north of the Tropic of Capricorn, 80 km northeast off the coast of Gladstone, access via Gladstone Airport to Heron by 30 minute helicopter flight, 45 minute boat transfer from Heron Island to Wilson Island.	Pike Withers	84
Australia	Uluru	Voyages Longitude 131° Uluru, Northern Territory Australia www.voyages.com.au	opened 2004 15 private luxury tents with king size beds, heating, air condition, private bathroom and shower restaurant, bar, situated on a sand dune close to the Uluru Kata Tjuta National Park, 6 km from Ayers Rock Airport.	Philip Cox	88
New Zealand	Wanaka	Whare Kea Lodge Mt Aspiring Road Wanaka 9192 New Zealand www.wharekealodge.com	opened 1998 2 suites and 4 rooms accommodating a maximum of 12 guests, all rooms with en suite bathrooms, double shower and sundeck, 3 lounge spaces including open fire, bar and dining area, massage room, cellar room, situated on the western shore of Lake Wanaka 7 km from Wanaka, 15 minutes flight to Wanaka.	Mayne & Bailieu Architects Inarc Design Group	92

hotel index

hotel index

Country / Location		Address	Information	Architecture & Design	Page
Tanzania	Mount Meru	Hatari Lodge Momella Arusha National Park Tanzania www.hatarilodge.com	opened 2004 9 rooms with their own private fireplace and terrace. Living and dining room, open fireplace, breakfast terrace, bar, library and wooden walkway for game viewing, located on the foot of Mount Meru, beyond Kilimandjaro at the northern edge of Arusha National Park.	Jörg & Marlies Gabriel with Remy Macha	120
Tanzania	Ngorongoro Crater	Ngorongoro Crater Lodge Ngorongoro Conservation Area, Tanzania www.ngorongorocrater.com	opened 1997 consists of 3 adjacent camps: North and South Camp with 12 suites each, Tree Camp with 6 suites, all accommodations with private viewing decks, dining room with fireplace, butler service, 1 hour drive from Olduvai.	Silvio Rech & Lesley Carstens Architecture and Interior Architecture	124
Botswana	Okavango Delta	Vumbura Plains Okovango Delta Vumbura Plains Botswana www.wilderness-safaris.com	opened 2005 2 camps linked by raised boardwalks, canvas tents under thatch with en suite facilities, fan, indoor and outdoor showers, dining, lounge and bar area in each camp, located in the north of Mombo, access only by aircraft into Vumbura airstrip and then by vehicle to camp, 40 minutes flight from Maun.	Silvio Rech & Lesley Carstens Architecture and Interior Architecture	128
Mozambique	Benguerra Island	Benguerra Lodge Benguerra Island Mozambique www.benguerra.co.za	opened 2003 11 chalets with en suite bathrooms and showers, 2 Honeymoon Suites with jacuzzi and plunge pool on a private deck, villa with personal chef, lounge, bar, dining room, library and large deck area, located within the Bazaruto Archipelago, 2 hours flight from Johannesburg International Airport, a short boat ride from Vilanculos.	Trevor Landrey	134
Namibia	Damaraland	Mowani Mountain Camp Twyfelfontein Damaraland Namibia www.mowani.com	opened 2000 12 luxury tents on wooden platforms with en suite bathroom and veranda, 1 luxury room with en suite bathroom and private terrace, 1 luxury suite with bedroom, lounge, indoor and outdoor shower, terrace and private butler service, open air lounge, bar, Rock Pool 15 minutes drive from private airstrip.	Andre Louw Klaus Brandt	138

hotel index

architects & designers

photo credits

all other photos by
Roland Bauer, Michelle Galindo and Martin Nicholas Kunz

imprint

Bibliographic information published by Die Deutsche Bibliothek. Die Deutsche Bibliothek lists this publication in the Deutsche Nationalbibliografie; detailed bibliographic data are available on the internet at http://ddb.de
ISBN 10: 3-89986-071-3
ISBN 13: 978-3-89986-071-9

1st edition

Printed in Austria
by Vorarlberger Verlagsanstalt AG, Dornbirn

Editors | Martin Nicholas Kunz, Patricia Massó
Editorial coordination | Hanna Martin
Copy editing | Rosina Geiger
Translations | LingServe Ltd, www.lingserve.com

Layout | Hanna Martin, Alexander Storck
Imaging | Jan Hausberg

avedition GmbH
Königsallee 57 | 71638 Ludwigsburg | Germany
p +49-7141-1477391 | f +49-7141-1477399
www.avedition.com | kontakt@avedition.com

Further information and links at
www.bestdesigned.com
www.fusion-publishing.com

Texts (pages) | Frank Bantle (8, 50, 58, 100), Frank Deppe (28), Marei Drassdo (36, 92, 156), Katharina Feuer (40, 62, 106, 120, 124, 128, 142, 152), Rosina Geiger (134), Isabella Kempf (112, 116), Vanessa Krestel (146), Martin Nicholas Kunz (22), Patricia Massó (138), Veronika Pfeiffer (80), Erika Ranft (18, 96), Tanja Schuler (12, 68), Heinfried Tacke (introduction, 32, 46, 54, 72, 76, 84, 88)

Special thanks to Anke Schaffelhuber from Wilderness Safaris for her expert advise, as well as Sandra Beltran, Ikal del Mar | Alain Castaneda, Reserva Amazónica Lodge | Frédéric Coustols, Castelnau des Fieumarcon | Alicia Fernández, Son Bernadinet | Marlies Gabriel, Hatari Lodge | Maria Reischl, Arabella Sheraton Hotels | Neil Rogers, Blancaneaux | Germán del Sol, Remota | Raffaella Geddes, Whitepod | Damien Hanger, Voyages | Vanessa Hauser, Smart Partners | Roland Hoede, Exclusive Travel Choice | Ian Hunter, Tsala Treetop Lodge | Josef Innerhofer, Pergola Residence | Ingo Jacob, Travel Consultants Africa | Heinz Legler, Verana | Liesl Liebenberg, Visions of Africa | Veronique Lièvre, Verana | Corinne Maloney, Daintree Eco Lodge & Spa | Fabrizio Molinaro, Alfajiri Villas | Samir Saab, Ikal del Mar | Isabell Schreml, zfl Munich | Panida Somton, Kirimaya | Marlene Songin, Verana | Elizabeth Worton, Eco Tulum Resorts for their support.

Martin Nicholas Kunz
1957 born in Hollywood. Founder of fusion publishing creating content for architecture, design, travel, and lifestyle publications.

Patricia Massó
1962 born in Stuttgart. Working as marketing and PR consultant with an emphasis on hotel business and editor of several hotel and design books.

best designed:
outdoor living
modular houses
hotel pools

best designed hotels:
Asia Pacific
Americas
Europe I (urban)
Europe II (countryside)

best designed wellness hotels:
Asia Pacific
Americas
Europe
Africa & Middle East

All books are released in German and English